WRITING A
RESEARCH PAPER

Lionel Menasche

Pitt Series in English as a Second Language

Ann Arbor *city (place of publish.)*

THE UNIVERSITY OF MICHIGAN PRESS

First publish,

''The Challenge to Intelligence Testing in Schools'' is reprinted from N. L. Gage and David C. Berliner, *Educational Psychology*, pp. 233–35. Copyright © 1979 by Houghton Mifflin Company. Used by permission. ''Gifted Pupils: Many Are Unidentified, Underserved'' is reprinted with permission from EDUCATION WEEK, Volume 1, Number 42, September 1, 1982. ''What Kind of Place is a University?'' is reprinted by permission of Herbert A. Simon from *The Pittsburgh Undergraduate Review*, 1981, 2(1). Extracts from ''The Aims and Purposes of the Research Paper,'' by R. A. Schwegler and L. K. Shamoon, are reprinted from *College English*, 1982, *44*, pp. 817–824.

For Felicity, Renee, and Edward

Contents

Preface

This textbook has been designed to help ESL students write a research paper. It can also be used by native English-speaking students. The process has been divided into steps, with specific assignment instructions for each. By concentrating on each step separately, the overall process becomes less difficult for students who have never before written a research paper. Those who are familiar with the process, because they have written one in another language, will find this set of assignments and exercises to be a useful way of adapting their accustomed writing conventions to a form acceptable in English.

Other special features that characterize this guide are the use of ESL peer models as an encouragement to ESL writers; cross-cultural awareness, reflected in careful explanation of culturally determined issues such as plagiarism; simplicity of language of explanation wherever this is achievable without oversimplifying the concepts; an extensive specialized glossary; and a steady insistence on the fact that the writing process is recursive, open-ended, and generative of ideas.

The attempt to include these features and the use of a step by step approach are essential in changing the research paper writing task from a daunting, anxiety-ridden experience into a manageable and even interesting learning and self-expression activity.

Acknowledgments

This guide owes much to the way research paper writing has been taught for some years in the English Language Institute, University of Pittsburgh. It also owes much to Mary N. Bruder and Christina B. Paulston, Co-Directors of the Institute, who encouraged its production.

Students and teachers in the Institute have made valuable suggestions for improvements of various kinds. I thank them. I am especially grateful to the students who gave permission for their research paper work to be quoted as examples.

My special thanks also go to Fran Williams, who somehow manages to combine typing at the speed of light with accuracy; to Michael Joyce, of the University of Pittsburgh Press, who has done sterling work in editing a difficult manuscript; and to Pat Furey, of the English Language Institute, for valuable assistance with proofreading.

For stimulating my interest in the teaching of composition, I am indebted to Anthony R. Petrosky, David Bartholomae, William L. Smith, and William E. Coles, all of the University of Pittsburgh.

To the Teacher

This textbook can be used in various ways: as part of a general writing course, as the focus of a course that teaches only the writing of research papers, as a reference book for individual students, or as a supplementary text in any academic course in which students inexperienced in the activity are required to write a research paper. The exact method of using it must of course be determined separately for each teaching situation.

The units which contribute directly to writing the research paper are arranged in the following way:

1. An assignment instruction is given, separated from the rest of the unit by lines. The series of assignments should be followed in sequence to build up into a complete research paper.

2. The assignment instruction is followed by some supporting explanation and, where necessary, examples designed to help the writer fulfill the requirements of that unit's assignment.

3. Exercises are provided for many of the units.

Units 1, 5, 9, 16, 17, and 18, which do not begin with assignment instructions, provide supplementary but important information. Two of these units (5 and 9) include exercises.

The following general procedure has been found to be effective for class use of a typical work unit:

1. Assign the unit to be read as homework.

2. If there is an assignment instruction for that unit, read it aloud in class. Mention the due date for the assignment. Discuss any points that the students ask about. When the unit is not one with an assignment, a similar homework reading and classroom discussion routine can still be followed.

3. Do any exercises in the unit, either in class or partly in class and partly as homework. Complete these exercises before the students work on the assignment. (It is not necessary to do all the exercises with all students; instructors should select those that will be most useful for each particular group.)

4. Take in the completed assignment for the unit. Check or grade it in relation to how well it contributes to the overall research paper writing process. Points may be assigned to each step to ensure that student effort is distributed fairly evenly over the whole process. (See Appendices I and II.)

5. If the checking or grading shows up matters that are difficult for many students, discuss these in class, referring again to relevant explanations and exercises in the unit.

6. For difficulties that are not general, write comments on the assignment or discuss the problems with individual students outside class.

7. Request assignment revisions as necessary.

UNIT 1
Writing Research Papers

An extremely common requirement of many academic courses is the "research" or "term" paper. It is a lengthy written composition that is usually developed and written during the course of a whole term or semester. In essence, it involves the writer in searching for published information on a specific topic, studying and thinking about this information, and then writing about the topic in a way that makes use of the information. It is an activity which many ESL students are unfamiliar with. Most are unfamiliar with the English language conventions that are involved, even when they have written such papers in their own language.

Research papers are a standard student and scholarly activity, because they demonstrate that the writer has read widely in a certain subject area (implying familiarity with library resources), assimilated and thought critically about the reading, and, finally, written a fully documented exposition of the issues.

TYPES OF RESEARCH PAPER

In its broadest sense, the term "research" simply means scholarly or scientific investigation or inquiry. When applied to a student's work for a particular paper, the term can mean one of two things:

1. Gathering information on a topic from several sources and presenting it in one's own words in a coherent, organized way. In this type, the writer just reports what others have said, *without* making any attempt to add personal comments or a personal point of view on the main issue. This is a common requirement of undergraduate courses and is often called a "report."

2. When the writer presents the ideas of others and also makes judgments on them, adds personal comments, and tries to *support a different, personal position* on the main issue, the paper is an "argumentative" one. (It is sometimes called a "thesis.") In graduate courses, this is the standard requirement. This is also the type of paper that scholars publish in journals, because it is this type that communicates advances in knowledge, new ideas, and new points of view. Sometimes this type of paper forms the basis of a "proposal" (as for a graduate thesis or dissertation), because it concludes with a statement of a proposed project that the writer or someone else will undertake.

1

STEPS IN WRITING A RESEARCH PAPER

A look at the contents page of this book will give you a rough idea of some of the stages you must go through in producing a research paper. The following chart will give you a more detailed picture.

Choose a subject.
↓
Is it practical and interesting?
    Yes   No ——————
↓
Check reference sources for your topic in the library.
↓
Narrow the subject. ←——————
↓
Is it narrow enough?
    Yes   No ——————
↓
Find out what resources the library has for this topic by beginning a preliminary bibliography.
↓
Are there useful books and articles available?
    Yes   No   ——————
↓
Further develop a preliminary bibliography.
↓
Read and take notes to get familiar with the topic. ←——————
↓
Do you know enough to be able to focus on one, very limited aspect?
    Yes   No   ——————
↓
Develop a preliminary thesis statement and preliminary outline.
↓
Continue reading and taking notes. ←——————
↓
Do you have enough notes, information, and ideas?
    Yes   No   ——————
↓
Revise your preliminary thesis statement and preliminary outline.
↓
Draft the body of the paper.
↓

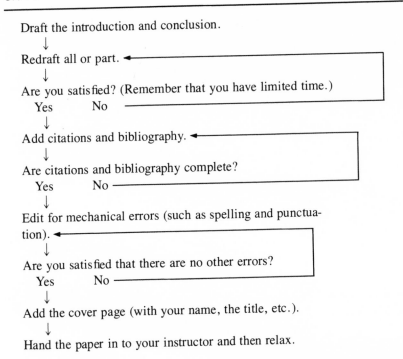

Draft the introduction and conclusion.
↓
Redraft all or part. ◄───────────────────────────────┐
↓   │
Are you satisfied? (Remember that you have limited time.) │
  Yes   No ─────────────────────────────────┘
↓
Add citations and bibliography. ◄───────────────────┐
↓   │
Are citations and bibliography complete?   │
  Yes   No ───────────────────────────────────┘
↓
Edit for mechanical errors (such as spelling and punctua-
tion). ◄──┐
↓   │
Are you satisfied that there are no other errors? │
  Yes   No ───────────────────────────────────┘
↓
Add the cover page (with your name, the title, etc.).
↓
Hand the paper in to your instructor and then relax.

What is shown in this chart may seem quite complicated, but if you think about each step separately and concentrate on that step alone, you will be surprised at how you get through it all quite easily. Do not think too much about the final product or about the whole process that takes so many weeks. Certainly you should keep these in mind in a general way, so that you know where you are going and how to get there, but concentrate on each step separately as you go along, and your research paper writing will not be so difficult after all.

THE STRUCTURE OF RESEARCH PAPERS

Regardless of subject area, most research papers have a similar general structure.

The introductory paragraphs state what is to be discussed and give the context of the subject, normally mentioning work done by others. The introduction then usually mentions how the writer will deal with the subject, whether by summarizing and synthesizing the work of others (a report), or by arguing logically about facts and theories, or by presenting the results of experimental research, or in any other way or combination of ways. The end of the introduction usually includes the main idea sentence (or thesis statement).

The longest section of a research paper is usually called the "body" to distinguish it from the introduction and conclusion. It consists of many paragraphs, carefully linked with the introduction and conclusion and with each other, which present information and discussion in an organized way.

The concluding paragraphs usually summarize the main points of the paper and restate, in different wording, the thesis statement. Often the conclusion also has some indication of the implications and consequences of the study, such as a recommendation for action or further research.

Choosing a Subject

Assignment

Decide on a subject that you want to write about, but at this first stage do not narrow it down too much. Make a note of it on a sheet of paper and add a few sentences explaining why you want to work on this particular subject. Turn it in to your instructor by the due date.

There are two guiding principles to remember when choosing something to write about: practicality and interest.

Because you have a limited time to work in, you must be sure that there will be adequate information available to you in your college library or from local libraries and information sources. This is usually not a problem for most students in selecting a subject. If you are taking a course in biology, for instance, the general subject area will usually be well represented in the libraries. If the course is a more specialized one within biology, in cell biology or lipids, for example, there will still be basic reference materials available in most libraries. However, when the subject area is not dictated by the course, there may be a problem. If you are considering writing about some aspect of your home country, perhaps its history, you should not assume that there will be enough information available locally. A preliminary survey of local resources is essential in such a case.

Interest, as well as practicality, is important because you will be working with this subject for many weeks. If you do not have a real interest in it, you may lose motivation at some stage and this will make your task much harder. A common and realistic question students frequently ask at this stage is, ''How will I know that I can maintain interest in the subject until I have studied it thoroughly? It seems that I must study it to know if I want to study it!'' There is no simple answer to this question. One of the aims of the research paper is to provide the opportunity for you to gain a deep understanding of the subject. Usually, the more one gets into a subject, the more interesting it becomes. In general, you should select something that seems to promise real value to you, perhaps something that you have always wanted to learn more about but have lacked the opportunity to, or possibly a subject you know will be valuable to you later in your more specialized academic work.

Examples: Choosing a subject

EXAMPLE 1 (Ghareeb Ghareeb)

The topic is an investigation of the relationship between depression and assertiveness. I have chosen this topic because I
will use it for my dissertation, and it is something that
interests me.

EXAMPLE 2 (Synian Hwang)

Topic: In the subject area of statistics--some aspects of the
theoretical developments in sampling theorem.

Explanation of choice: I am interested in the subject.

EXAMPLE 3 (Boshin Lin)

Topic: Computer applications in Biological Science.

Why? Because my college major was Biology and now I am
majoring in Information Science, which uses the computer as a
basic tool. I have chosen this topic, hoping it will relate
these two majors.

UNIT 3
Using the Library

If you have never written a research paper before, you may be surprised at how much time you spend in the library finding relevant materials. You will move many times between the card catalog, the reference area, the indexes, the book stacks, the periodicals room, and possibly the microform readers. You will also have to talk to the librarians a number of times. The process may seem complicated at first, but all it takes to become familiar with a library is some practice. The following library exercises will give you just the practice you need. Do them as directed by your instructor—some in class, some for homework, and most of them in the library. Your instructor or a librarian may give you an orientation tour of the library, but after that you should never hesitate to ask one of them for help. As an information sheet for students in one university library (University of Pittsburgh, Hillman Library) puts it:

> *Do not be afraid to ask for help.* While the REFERENCE LIBRARIANS will not choose a topic for you, or determine which aspect of a topic you should explore, they will help you to identify your interest and to select opening sets of terms. If you are unsure about how to choose, narrow, and refine your topic; if you are not sure where to begin or how to proceed; if you do not understand the organization of a source (e.g., card catalog, bibliography, index, etc.), or the meaning of certain symbols or abbreviations, ASK A REFERENCE LIBRARIAN. Try them. You'll like them!

Do not expect that all your walking about in the library will always lead you to the books and articles you are looking for. Part of the initial research activity is almost always frustration at not finding what you want. Keep on looking until you are certain that the materials are not available for your topic and only then consider changing to a topic for which information is more easily available.

LIBRARY OF CONGRESS CALL NUMBER

The "call number" of a book in a library is the number which is written on the spine of the book and on its card (top left corner) in the card catalog. It is the number you use in order to locate the book on the library shelves. The Library of Congress numbering system and the Dewey decimal system are the most common types of numbering. The Library of Congress system is gradually taking over as the most used one in college libraries, so it is the one discussed here.

Here is an example for the book *Thought and Language* by L. S. Vygotsky:

P 105	——————— class number
V 996	——————— author number
1962	——————— date for later editions

} call number

Here, the P stands for the general subject area (in this case, Language and Literature) and the 105 is a sequence of numbers for further subdivisions of the class number. Sometimes the class number starts with two letters, with the second letter referring to a subdivision of the subject. The V is the first part of the author number (also called the book number). The book number usually starts with the first letter of the author's last name (in this case, Vygotsky) and this letter is followed by a number sequence for further subdivision of the book category. The third line in this example is the date of this edition of the book (in this case, 1962). The date is not usually included for the first edition of the book but only for later editions. When you are looking for books, you must be sure to copy out *exactly* the *whole* call number, keeping the letters and numbers in the right order and keeping each line separate. Then follow the principles of ''top to bottom'' (for each line) and ''left to right'' (within each line).

To find a book, follow these steps:

1. Start on the left of the class number to find the area of the library shelves where books with the first letter are located.

2. Work from left to right. If there is then another letter, find its shelf location *within* the area indicated by the first letter.

3. Then work from left to right with the numerals of the first line to locate the area of each numeral in turn. The numerals, referring to subsections, become more specific as you work through them.

4. Next, move to the second line, the author number. Again work from left to right, taking each letter and numeral in turn, one at a time. Again, you will be getting more and more specific and, if the book is on the shelf (not out on loan and not out of position), you should find it when you reach the last numeral.

Note:

(a) If you see a small ''q'' or ''f'' before the class number, this means that the book is a larger size (''quarto'' or ''folio'') and is in a different section of the library. Ask a librarian about the location.

(b) Sometimes, after the author number or date, you will see a small ''c'' with a number on it. This simply means ''copy'' and refers to how many copies are in the library (for example, ''c2'' means ''second copy'').

(c) Sometimes, for extra subdivision, the class number has two lines, or the author number has an extra letter among the numerals, or a line has a decimal point in it. In all these cases, all you must do is follow the usual ''top to bottom'' and ''left to right'' rules.

Exercises: Using the library

(Numbers 1–5 can be done in class)

1. Choose any *two* or *three* books that you have in class, or that your teacher brings to class. Study their title pages and copyright pages in order to find the author's name, full title, year of publication, and publisher.

2. Study the example below of a card from the library card catalog. Prepare as much as possible of a similar card for a textbook that you are now using in your reading or writing class. (Note that the example is of an author card. A *subject* card or a *title* card looks the same except that the title or subject is typed at the top of the card.) You will find bibliographical information on the title page of a book and on the copyright page, which is often on the reverse of the title page. Which pieces of information are you unable to get from the book itself?

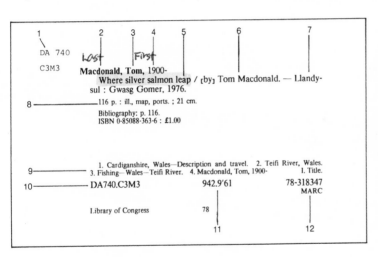

1. Call number (Library of Congress classification). ②Author's last name. 3. Author's first name. 4. Author's date of birth. 5. Book title. 6. Author's name (first name, then last name). 7. Place of publication, publisher, and date. 8. Physical make-up of book. 9. Additional cards under these headings (cross-references). 10. Library of Congress classification. 11. Dewey decimal classification. 12. Library of Congress card number.

3. (a) Alphabetize the family names of all the students in your class.

(b) Alphabetize the following according to family names. When two last names are the same, use the first name's initials for further alphabetization. In this exercise, when the last name includes separate elements such as "van der," "von," "de," "el," "Al," treat these elements as part of the last name only when you know that this is how the name is usually alphabetized or when the parts of the name are joined by a hyphen or apostrophe. (There is a lot of variation in the way libraries treat these names. So, when searching for references in a library, look under both parts of the last name if you cannot find a reference where you expect it to be.) For most Oriental names the family name is written first, so use the first one you read for alphabetization.

Thomas Lee Crowell, Helen Barnard, Caroll Washington Pollock, Fraida Dubin, Elite Olshtain, Marcella Frank, Robert G. Bander, Edward T. Hall, George Orwell, Alan T. Hall, Frank d'Angelo, Ali el-Osman, Hendrik van der Merwe, Heinz von Loringhoven, Albert Peter Hall, Mohammed al-Arabi, Pierre de Proyart, Jaime de los Rios, John Smith, James R. Smith, Xavier Ortega, Mao Tse-Tung, Wang Minn-Hu, Matsushita Yoko, P. R. O'Hara, F. Williams, P. George Zelman, JoEllen Walker, Hamish Angus McTaggart, Peter P. Peterkin.

4. Look at this call number and answer the questions that follow it.

> BV5077
>
> R9
>
> F2
>
> 1978
>
> c14

(a) What is the general subject area, represented by B? (Refer to glossary, under "Library of Congress," in this textbook.)

(b) The author's name is Fedotov. Which line is the author number?

(c) Do you think this is the first edition of this book?

(d) The library has many copies of this book. At least how many do you think it has?

5. Study the following labelled extract from the *Readers' Guide to Periodical Literature* and then answer the questions that follow.

1. Subject headings.
2. Cross references.
3. Subject subheadings. 4. Cross reference.

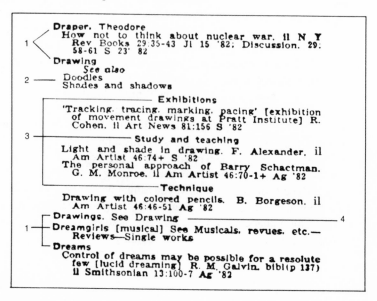

One article entry from the above extract:

```
                           1                    2          3
                          /                     \          |
     Light and shade in drawing.  F.  Alexander.  il
       Am  Artist  46:74+  S  '82
          4/       5/     \6  \7  \8
```

1. Article title. 2. Author's name. 3. Abbreviation for "illustrated." 4. Abbreviated name of journal. 5. Volume. 6. Page number. 7. Abbreviation for month of publication. 8. Abbreviation for year of publication.

(a) What is the name of an author who wrote an article on dreams?

(b) When did R. Cohen publish an article in *Art News*?

(c) What is the title of an article by B. Borgeson?

(d) Under what other subject headings can you find entries on the musical "Dreamgirls"?

(e) On which pages of *Smithsonian* magazine, volume 13, will you find an article on dreams?

(f) Is the article by F. Alexander in the journal, *American Artist*, illustrated?

6. Choose *one* of the following authors: Pablo Neruda, William Shakespeare, Khalil Gibran. Look in the card catalog to see which of this author's works are available in the library. Remember that they are all alphabetized by author's <u>last</u> name. Note the call numbers of *one* or *two* of the writer's works and be sure that you know where to find them on the library shelves. If they are not on the shelves, find out why by asking a librarian. Write down and hand in to your instructor the author's name, the title(s), and call number(s).

7. Locate the reference section in the library. Find *two* different sets of multivolume encyclopedias (such as the *Encyclopedia Americana* or *Encyclopaedia Britannica*). Compare their entries on your country or your city. At the end of each entry is there a bibliography? If so, select *one* book listed in these bibliographies and check in the card catalog to see whether the library has it. If the library does not have it, try to find one of the listed books that *is* available in the library.

8. Use the card catalog subject entries to find out if the library has any books on *one* or *two* of the following subjects:

gemstones	solar energy
twins	Spanish poetry
impressionist art	Bali
spices	U.S. relations with Africa
mysticism	Hawaii
biogenetic engineering	language teaching

Notice whether any of the cards say "See" or "See also" followed by an extra reference. Follow up this cross reference by looking for it in the appropriate place in the card catalog.

9. Locate the *Readers' Guide to Periodical Literature*. Find an entry for *one article* on any *one* of the subjects listed in Exercise 8. (Note that this does *not* ask you to find a subject entry, but only an entry for one *article* from a periodical.) Copy down the entry exactly as it appears. Then rewrite the entry *without using any abbreviations at all*. For this you will have to refer to the explanation of abbreviations at the front of each volume. (For example, "D," in nonabbreviated form, will be *December*.)

10. Find any specialized index for a subject that you are interested in. Select an entry for *one* article. Copy it out in the way it appears and then in nonabbreviated form.

11. For *one* article in the *Readers' Guide to Periodical Literature* and for *one* in a more specialized index, note the following information:

author, title, name of journal (periodical), volume number, page numbers, date of publication.

12. For *both* of the periodicals you noted in Exercise 11, determine whether the library has them by consulting the list of periodicals stocked by the library. Then find the location of the periodicals, if they are available, and look in the specific volume you noted to find the article. At the end of the article you may find a bibliography that you could use to follow up further references on the same topic. Is there one?

◫▭▷ UNIT 4
Narrowing the Focus

Assignment

Work out which specific aspect of your subject area you will investigate and write about. That is, narrow down or limit the focus of interest. Make a note of this limited topic on a sheet of paper and turn it in to your instructor. Add a few sentences explaining why this narrow issue is the one you want to work on and in what way it is narrow enough. To make this last point clear, contrast it with a broader issue within the same subject area or explain how you have narrowed it down.

A suitably narrow or limited topic to do research on is always worked out after very careful thought and, unless you are already familiar in some detail with the subject, you will probably discover as you begin to do the research that you have not limited it enough. This should not be regarded as an anxiety-causing problem. In fact, it is part of the interest of the activity. You undertake research to find out what you do not know, and it is part of the satisfaction of finding out and learning when you realize how much has already been written on your topic.

At this stage, you do not abandon the general topic and look for another. If it attracted you in the first place, you should survey what has so far been published. Then ask yourself whether you could select one of the issues discussed in these publications as the focus of your paper. You may find that some of the authorities on the subject disagree with each other on certain points. If so, these points, or one of them, may provide you with a topic to pursue further.

Consider this example: A student of African history may start out with the history of British colonialism as a general subject area. After reading a little in this area, the subject could be narrowed down to research on why the British gradually withdrew from their African colonies during the last thirty years. After further reading, the same subject could be limited even more, possibly to a study of one or two countries. Even further restriction of the subject could be necessary. For example, historians may disagree about why the British withdrew from their African colonies—so the research paper writer may decide to investigate which of these historians' theories seems to provide the best explanation in regard to only one country.

Examples: Narrowing the focus of a subject

EXAMPLE 1 (Ghareeb Ghareeb)

The topic is an investigation of the relationship between depression and assertiveness in an Eastern population.

The relationship between depression and assertiveness in Western culture has been confirmed. I am going to research the same relationship between the two variables in Eastern culture. The purpose of the study is to find out the kind of relationship between depression and assertiveness in an Egyptian population.

EXAMPLE 2 (Synian Hwang)

Topic: Some aspects of the theoretical developments in sampling theorem under finite population model.

Since the sampling theorem is too broad, I will concentrate my attention on the finite population model. Under this model, I will study some results from a theoretical point of view.

EXAMPLE 3 (Yehuda Beneduardo)

Topic: The use of audio-visual aids in language teaching.

Narrowing the focus: At first I thought of writing about the use of the language laboratory, but a lot has already been done on that, especially on the use of videotapes with audiotapes. So I will narrow it to a new experimental field, which is the use of microcomputers in a language laboratory, because there are some disagreements about how they can be used. Some people say that they are hard for students to use and still too expensive.

Exercises: Narrowing the focus of a subject

1. General subjects: computer science; hunting; card games; art; education; health; world languages; animals.

Select one of the above subjects and narrow it down in stages, getting more and more specific at each stage, until you have limited it enough to make it suitable for a short research paper.

Example

General Subject:	Health
Narrowed:	Health maintenance.
Narrowed further:	Health maintenance in children.
Narrowed further:	Education for children about health maintenance.

Narrowed further:	Problems and solutions in educating children about health maintenance.
Narrowed further:	The use of television cartoons as a means of educating children about health maintenance.
Narrowed further:	The most effective type of television cartoon for educating children about health maintenance.

2. Select any general subject you are interested in. Narrow it down stage by stage (as in the example in Exercise 1). Write down the subject and each stage of narrowing, to hand in to your instructor. Be sure that the final step is limited enough for a student to handle in a short research paper.

▱▱▱ UNIT 5
Preliminary Survey of Reference Sources

Assignment

Go to the library (or to more than one, as needed) and find out what reference sources will help you to trace books and articles on your topic. *List them* and hand the list in to your instructor by the due date. The first thing on all lists will be the card catalog. Indexes to journal and magazine articles will also appear on all lists. Other sources may be bibliographies attached to important works—books or articles—in the subject area. (Note that this assignment does *not* ask for the titles of the books and articles you will actually use, but only for the reference sources that will help you find them.)

An essential step at the beginning of your research is to find out what reference sources are available in your subject area. These are indexes, catalogs, bibliographies, compilations of abstracts, and any other library materials that will guide you to books and articles on your chosen subject.

Your first stop should be the card catalog. Here, look up all the headings and subheadings that relate to your potential project. You may find very many entries. If so, the subheadings and book titles may give you a clue on ways to limit the topic. Cross-references in the catalog will lead you to other related material. As you proceed with this make a note of all the words and short phrases that describe aspects of your subject. This will be your set of "search terms." Different indexes may use slightly different terms (also called "descriptors"). You can also use the *Directory of Library of Congress Subject Classifications* as a source of search terms. (Copies of this volume are usually located near the card catalog or at the library's reference desk.)

Although you should start with the card catalog, it is never enough as a source of information for references. Its subject headings refer only to books, not articles.

To write an up-to-date paper, you will need to decide on what recent articles to read. To find out about these, you should study bibliographical indexes, both the general ones and those which are specific to your subject area. The reference librarians will help you find these. Usually, the first general one you are shown will be the *Readers' Guide to Periodical Literature,* which covers articles in the more popular magazines. Others, of a more scholarly type might include the *Humanities Index* and *Social Science Index*.

If you don't know the indexes for your subject, ask a librarian for the *Guide to Reference Books* (edited by Gordon Sheehy). This will help you discover relevant indexes and other reference materials. Another guide to finding such materials is the *Bibliographic Index*, which lists books and journal articles that have bibliographies. Also, it is now becoming very common for researchers to conduct computerized searches of bibliographic data bases. Most large college libraries have such facilities and the search is often free. Some computer searches provide abstracts of the articles in addition to title, author, and publication details.

Finally, it is important to remember that people, as well as books and computers, can be used to obtain bibliographic information. This is especially important for graduate students and is often the quickest way to find recent and useful articles and books. Approach your professors and advanced graduate students in your subject and ask them to refer you to recent books or survey articles. They will probably also be helpful in telling you about the relevant indexes in your field or about other ways of obtaining bibliographic information.

Once you are familiar with the materials that will lead you to relevant book and articles, you can begin to work on the next stage—the preparation of a preliminary bibliography. At this point you can return to the card catalog to use it for its main function—indicating by means of its call numbers what books are located in the library.

Examples: Lists of reference sources

A. This example is for a research paper on a topic in the sociology of education.

1. Card catalog.
2. Readers' Guide to Periodical Literature.
3. Social Sciences Index.
4. Popular Periodicals Index.
5. Sociology of Education Abstracts.
6. Bibliography in a book of readings: *Education and Sociology,* P. Jones (ed.).

B. These reference sources are for a paper in chemistry.

1. Card catalog.
2. Applied Science and Technology Index.
3. Chemical Abstracts.
4. Library Guide for the Chemist.
5. Encyclopedia of Science and Technology.

C. For this list, the topic is in the field of art.
  1. Card catalog.
  2. Encyclopedia of World Art.
  3. The American Library Compendium and Index of World Art.
  4. Ceramic Abstracts.
  5. The Art Index.
  6. Guide to Art Reference Books.

◻◫▷ UNIT 6
Preliminary Bibliography

Assignment

Prepare a preliminary bibliography for your research paper. This bibliography is a list of available books and articles that you think will be useful sources of information and ideas when writing the paper. Follow these guidelines:

1. Include books *and* articles.
2. Document each item on a separate file card.
3. Prepare at least ten such cards (preferably more).
4. Note the call number for each reference on its card.
5. When you hand in your set of cards to your instructor, add an extra card on top with your name on it and the heading:
   Preliminary Bibliography.
6. On the top card also write down which bibliographical style guide you are following. If you follow the examples in this unit, write: Style guide: *Publication Manual of the American Psychological Association*. If you arrange with your instructor that you will follow another guide, such as the *Modern Language Association Style Sheet* or Kate L. Turabian's *A Manual for Writers of Term Papers, Theses and Dissertations*, give your instructor a photocopied page showing a sample of the style you will use. Whichever style you choose, be consistent: follow *only* that style in *all* your research paper documentation.

To prepare a preliminary bibliography you must work in the library with the indexes relevant to your field and with the card catalog. You will also get ideas for this preliminary list from the references and bibliographies given in books and articles that are closely connected with your topic.

The preparation of this list is an on-going process. Once you begin to read for information in the material that you find, you will come across other references. However, at the very beginning of the search for information, you should simply list whatever may seem relevant. Then, when you have an initial ten or so items on your list, check to see whether they are locally available. At this point in the process, you should try to find the items in the main college libraries, on the shelves, to ensure that they are available. Many of the relevant references may not be held by the library, others may be lost, and others may be out on loan and difficult to get back in time for you to use. When you do find some of the items, take a quick look at their bibliographies to see if they yield further titles for your search; if so, follow those up too. You do not need to begin the detailed reading of your books and articles at this point, but it is necessary to skim the material very quickly to be sure that is relevant to your topic.

Expect to spend several hours going back and forth between the indexes, card catalogs, shelves, and, if necessary (it generally is for researchers), the librarians, who will help when something is difficult for you to find. If something is listed in the card catalog, it should be either in the library or out on loan; if not, consult the librarian. Some libraries maintain a computerized list of what is out on loan. You can usually consult such lists without first asking a librarian.

Sometimes you will find that your initial judgment of what seemed useful is wrong, because you were able to judge only from the title or an abstract (a summary of the content of a book or article). Items that you quickly skim and find irrelevant should not be included in the preliminary bibliography that you give to your instructor, which should contain only those items definitely relevant and available to you. Remember that it is not necessarily the case that something will be available just because it is in the card catalog; you must ensure that it is there by checking on the shelves.

When you begin to look in the card catalog and in journal indexes for references, you may find that there is a very large number of them related to your topic. In such a situation, it is certainly the case that your topic is still not narrow enough. For the limited time available for a student paper, you must have a topic that is extremely limited in range. One approximate indication that it is really limited enough is that you will find only a few references directly related to your topic, although there may be many that are indirectly related.

USING FILE CARDS

You may ask why it is required in this assignment that you write each item of the bibliography on a separate card and not just as a list on a sheet of paper. A file card system is required because, as you will find, it is the most convenient one for later additions, removals, and alphabetizing of bibliographical items. In the end, it saves a great deal of time.

The size of the cards you use for this assignment does not really matter, but many students find it helpful to use small cards (3 × 5 or 4 × 6 inches) for this assignment and large cards (6 × 9 inches) for the later note taking assignment. The different sizes help you to avoid hunting for "lost" cards when the bibliography cards and note cards are all scattered on your desk. Some writers prefer to use file cards of different colors to differentiate bibliography from note cards.

Finally, remember to write down *all* the information about the publication, because you will thus save time later. You would not want to find at the last minute that you forgot to note the name of the publisher or the date of publication. Be complete now to avoid later frustration.

Examples: References in APA style

The rules and examples that follow are based on the style of the *Publication Manual of the American Psychological Association* (Third Edition, 1983), which is widely used in the social sciences, and which is becoming very popular in many other fields. Most of your citations will be of books and articles. The following points from the APA manual should be noted:

The last name (family name, surname) of each author is written first. (But do not do this with the name of an editor if that name is not in author position.)

Only the initials of the authors' and editors' first names are used, not the full first names.

The year of publication is placed in parentheses. (Add the month only when a periodical has no volume number.)

The title of an article is not underlined, but the name of a journal (periodical, magazine) is underlined or in italics.

The volume number of a journal is underlined or in italics.

The title of a book is underlined or in italics.

A standard article citation is in this order: author's name, date of publication, title of article, name of journal, volume number, page numbers of the article.

A standard book citation is in this order: author's name, date of publication, book title, place of publication, publisher.

Titles of books and articles in reference lists are not capitalized throughout; only the first letter of the first word, the first letter of the first word after a colon, and the first letter of a proper name are capitalized.

In the name of a journal, capitalize the first letter of the first word and the first letter of each major word. (Do not capitalize short prepositions, conjunctions, or articles, except when one is the first word of the journal's name.)

Punctuation, capitalization, underlining, and order of elements are important. Follow the forms carefully. Separate the four main parts of a citation (author, date, title, and publication details) with periods. Use commas within each part, except between place and publisher, where a colon is used. Extra information (such as edition number) is placed in parentheses.

When no author is given for a book or article, start with the title for alphabetization purposes.

An encyclopedia article is cited in the same way as an article in an edited book.

When no author is given, but there is a corporate author (such as a committee or association) or an editor, put the name of the corporate author or editor in author position for alphabetization purposes.

Indent three spaces every line after the first line of an entry.

Abbreviate the full name of the publishing company as much as possible by omitting initials and words such as ''company'' or ''corporation.'' (For example, write only ''Norton'' instead of ''W. W. Norton and Company.'')

Instead of ''and,'' use the symbol ''&'' in the reference list.

EXAMPLE 1: Book Reference

1. Capitalize first letter of name. 2. Author's last name. 3. Initial of author's first name. 4. Date of publication, in parentheses. 5. Capitalize first letter of first word. 6. Book title, underlined. 7. Indentation (three spaces). 8. Place of publication. 9. Name of publisher.

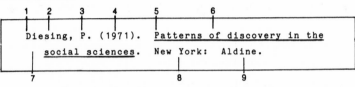

EXAMPLE 2: Article Reference

1. Author's last name. 2. Initials of author's first and middle names. 3. Date of publication. 4. Title of article, not underlined. 5. Name of journal, underlined. 6. Journal volume number, underlined. 7. Page numbers of the article.

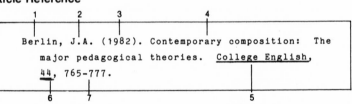

EXAMPLE 3: Preliminary Bibliography

The eleven cards shown on the following pages were produced by Ghareeb Ghareeb in response to the assignment instruction for this unit. Where there are no library call numbers in this preliminary bibliography, the card is for a journal article, or the student owns a personal copy of the book. The description beside each card indicates what kind it is.

```
          Preliminary Bibliography


             Ghareeb Ghareeb



      Style:  Publication Manual of
     the American Psychological Association
```

Top card for instruc-
tor's information
only

```
Alberti, R., & Emmons, M. (1973).  Your perfect right.
→ San Luis Obispo:  Impact.


  BF575
  A3A65
  1973
```

Book (two authors)

```
Beck, A.T. (1972).  Depression:  Causes and treatment.
  Philadelphia: ┘University of Pennsylvania
  Press.


  RC537
  B4
  1972
```

Book (one author)

**Article (two authors)
in an edited book
(two editors)**

Bellack, A.S., & Hersen, M. (1977). Self-report in-
ventories in behavioral assessment. In J.D.
Cone and R.P. Hawkins (Eds.), Behavioral
assessment: New directions in clinical
psychology (pp. 133-140). New York: Brunner/Mazel.

BF98.4
B34

**Article (one author)
in an edited book
(three editors)**

Cotler, S. (1976). Assertive training. In P. Binder,
S.A. Binder & B. Rimland (Eds.), Modern
therapies (pp. 26-43). Englewood Cliffs, NJ:
Prentice-Hall, 1976.

**Article (multiple au-
thors) in a journal**

Eisler, R.M., et al. (1973). Components of assertive
behavior. Journal of Clinical Psychology,
29, 295-299.

Eysenck, H.J. (1972). <u>Pyschology is about people</u>. LaSalle,
    IL: Library Press.

BF121
E94

Book (one author)

Farber, L. (1979, April). Merchandising depression.
    <u>Psychology Today</u>, pp. 63-64.

Article (one author)
in a journal using
date and no volume
number

Goodwin, F. (1974). On the biology of depression. In
    R. Friedman and M. Katz (Eds.), <u>The psychology</u>
    <u>of depression: Contemporary theory and research</u> (pp.
    231-251). New York: Wiley.

Article (one author)
in an edited book
(two editors)

Book (multiple authors)

```
Girinker, R.R., et al. (1961). The phenomena of
    depressions. New York: Harper.



RC518
G7
```

Abstract, from an index

```
Hayman, P.M. (1978). Effects on depression of assertion
    training. Dissertation Abstracts International,
    38, 501A.
```

FURTHER EXAMPLES OF THE APA STYLE

For types of citation not covered in these examples, consult the APA manual; graduate students should own a copy of this, or some other detailed style guide.

Buros, O. K. (ed.). (1972). *Mental Measurements Yearbook*. (7th ed.). Highland Park, NJ: Gryphon Press.

Annual publication (treated as a periodical)

Fitzgerald, S. M. (1973). *A career needs comparison of elementary school teachers and undergraduate students in an elementary school preparation program*. ERIC Document Reproduction Service No. ED 087 753.

Article in microform, from ERIC (Educational Resource Information Center)

DeVries, R., & Kohlberg, L. (1975, December). *Relations between Piagetian and psychometric assessment of intelligence.* Paper presented at the Piaget Symposium, Dallas, TX.

Conference paper (two authors)

Doherty, P. J. (1974). *Cognitive development of visually handicapped children.* Paper presented at the biennial conference of the Australian and New Zealand Association of Teachers of the Visually Handicapped, Queensland, Australia.

Conference paper (one author)

Howell, R. (1971). *Evaluation of cognitive abilities of emotionally disturbed children: An application of Piaget's theories.* Unpublished doctoral dissertation, Southern Illinois University.

Doctoral dissertation (unpublished, one author)

Newland, T. E. (1970). New developments in the intelligence testing of blind children. In L. L. Clark & Z. Z. Jastrzembska (eds.), *Proceedings of the Conference on New Approaches to the Evaluation of Blind Persons* (pp. 26–37). New York: American Foundation for the Blind.

Article (one author) in edited conference proceedings published as a book (two editors)

Simpkins, K., & Stephens, W. B. (1970). *Adaptation of Piagetian reasoning assessments for use with the visually handicapped.* Unpublished paper, Temple University.

Unpublished paper (two authors)

Stephens, W. B., & Sower, R. (1976). *The Philadelphia project: The analysis and development of reasoning.* Final Project Report, Grant No. 51-P-15497/3-02.

Project report (two authors)

Jones, S. P. (1983). A moving story. [Review of *See the dawn again* by J. McArthur.] *Modern Book Notes, 20,* 62–73.

Review of a book

The tree trunk. (1982, June 6). *Garden Magazine.* pp. 49–62, 73–74.

Magazine article (no author, no journal number, and discontinuous pages)

Exercises: Bibliographical citations

1. From the following statements about a book and an article, take the information you need for a complete citation of it in a bibliography.

(a) Recently I came across a useful book called *Research design and statistics for applied linguistics*. It was published by Newbury House and was written by two authors, Evelyn Hatch and Hossein Farhady. It was published in 1982. The publisher is located in Rowley, Massachusetts.

(b) I strongly advise you to read that article in the *History of Applied Technology Quarterly*. Its author is a famous researcher named I. M. Investigator. You'll find it between pages 119 and 123 in volume eighty-six. The title of the article is: Types of clay used in ancient Acapulcan pottery. It appeared in the journal in September, 1934.

2. In each of the following citations, *one* thing is *wrong* in order of elements or punctuation or capitalization or underlining/italics. Try to find what is wrong. Write out the corrected form. The first three citations can be found in correct form in the above examples. The next three have a clue to the error in parentheses.

(a) H. J. Eysenck. (1972). *Psychology is about people*. LaSalle, IL: Library Press.

(b) Farber, L. (1979, April). *Merchandising depression*. Psychology Today, 63–64.   Not I+I

(c) Goodwin, F. (1974). On the biology of depression. In R. Friedman & M. Katz (Eds.), *The Psychology of Depression: Contemporary Theory and Research*. New York: Wiley. (pp. -)

(d) Piaget, J. (1962). *The moral judgment of the child*. New York; Collier Books. (punctuation)

(e) Piaget, J. *Psychology of intelligence*. (1960). Paterson, NJ: Littlefield, Adams. (order of elements)

(f) Furth, H. G. (1966). Thinking without language. New York: Free Press. (underlining/italics)

(g) Jones, B. (1975). Spatial perceptions in the blind *British Journal of Psychology, 66*, 461–472.

(h) Henry, F. M. Reaction time—movement time correlations. *Perceptual and Motor Skills, 12*, 63–66.

(i) Singer, R. (1966). Interlimb skill ability in motor skill performance. *Research Quarterly, 37*, 406–410.

(j) Herzberg, F., Mausner, B., & Snyderman, B. (1959). *The motivation to work*. Wiley: New York.

(k) National Education Association. (1969). "Are teachers satisfied with their working conditions?" *NEA Research Bulletin, 47* (1), 6–7.

(l) Wolfe, S., & Wolfe, C. (1974). *Games without words*. Springfield, IL: Thomas.

3. For practice, write six bibliography cards together with other students in your class. (The books and articles for this exercise may be brought to class by the instructor or students.)

Remember that this unit refers only to the APA style. Other style guides have different forms of citation.

Capital

Hach E. & Farhady H. (1982) Research design and Statistics for applied linguistics. Rowley, Massachusetts : Newbury House.

I.M. (1934. Sep.) Types of clay used in ancient *investigator.* Acapulcan pottery. History of Applied Technology Quarterly. 86, 119-123.

Preliminary Thesis Statement

Assignment

Prepare a preliminary thesis statement for your research paper. It should express in *one sentence* the controlling idea of the whole paper.

For an argumentative paper, the thesis statement makes the claim that the paper tries to support with evidence.

For a report, it does not make a claim that needs proof; instead, the thesis statement is simply a statement describing the main idea or a question that will be answered by the information given in the paper.

Write down your thesis statement and hand it in to your instructor by the due date.

Even though the thesis statement is very short—just one sentence—it is very important and must be given a lot of thought, especially for an argumentative paper. The statement is called ''preliminary'' at this stage because you may find reason to change it as you proceed with your reading, note taking, and drafting.

To arrive at the thesis statement of an argumentative paper, you should first ask yourself: ''What do I want to prove? What is the key question that I want to answer?'' The reply to this will express your main purpose in writing the paper and will therefore provide the preliminary thesis statement. Remember these characteristics of an argumentative thesis statement:

(a) It is one sentence only.
(b) It makes a claim.
(c) Some people would disagree with the claim.
(d) Its main clause expresses the claim.
(e) Frequently, a subordinate part of the thesis statement expresses a contrasting viewpoint (for example, in a subordinate clause beginning with ''although'').

To arrive at a thesis statement for a report, simply ask yourself which area of information you wish to isolate and describe. The more general it is, the longer will be the report; the more specific and narrowed, the shorter it will be. For a one-semester report assignment, you should make it a very narrow topic. The thesis statement of a report has these qualities:

(a) It is one sentence only.

(b) Its main clause carries the main topic of the report.

Sometimes it is difficult to establish whether a thesis is an argumentative one or a report thesis. Your decision will depend on the context of the statement. For example, many years ago people were not sure if air pollution was linked to ill health, so, at that time, the thesis statement "air pollution is linked to ill health" would have been an excellent argumentative one. Nowadays, however, the same statement would be suitable for a report, not an argument, because the link between air pollution and ill health has been so well proven that no one would try to deny it.

Another way in which a thesis can be affected is by changing the social context in which it is applied. For instance, the thesis statement "Women teachers should be paid as much as men" is not a valid argumentative one when applied to the United States, where there is no discrimination on this issue in the teaching profession. Yet in some other countries men and women teachers are not paid the same for doing the same work, so the same sentence would, in reference to them, be a valid argumentative thesis statement.

Here are some examples of *argumentative thesis statements:*

Domiciliary treatment of tuberculosis has better results for the patients than isolation treatment within hospitals. (Ines Dourado)

This statement makes it clear that Ines will compare the results of the two ways of treating tuberculosis patients. She will aim to prove her assertion that one of them is better.

Coal is the best alternative as a substitute for oil in the near future. (Maite Terrer)

From this thesis statement we can see that Maite will discuss various alternatives to oil as a source of energy. She must prove her claim that coal is the best one.

Although many people believe that the realist method of staging is the best way to interpret a play, it is a limited form because art must recreate, not copy life. (Deolindo Checcucci)

To arrive at this thesis statement, Deolindo asked himself, "As an art form, what is the realist method of staging plays really like?" His answer was that it was limited, but he knew from his reading that many people believed it to be the best way to interpret a play. So his argument is given in the main clause (". . . it is a limited form . . .") and the opposite view is given in a subordinate clause ("Although many people believe . . ."). He has also added, in another subordinate clause, his reason for making the claim (". . . because art must . . .").

Although smokers and cigarette companies do not like to believe it, smoking is a clear cause of cancer. (Jehad Asfoura)

Jehad's question was "How strong is the connection between smoking and cancer?" He realized that some people (usually smokers, tobacco growers, and owners of cigarette companies) said there was no connection, others said there was a slight connection, and yet others said there was a strong connection. From his reading he was convinced that smoking is a clear cause of cancer, so his belief is given in the main clause of his thesis statement.

Here are two examples of *report thesis statements,* the ones that do not make a claim that must be proved:

Taking good photographs not only depends on having a camera, but also on combining the few fundamentals of color, light, weather conditions, techniques, and accessories. (Anavat Khavpatumthip)

This thesis statement tells the reader that Anavat's paper will describe the different things that need to be considered in taking photographs. There is no assertion here that needs argumentative proof because the paper will be reporting what is generally accepted by photographers. There is nothing controversial in the statement, nothing that an experienced photographer could disagree with.

Good nutrition, balanced diet, and exercise are important for good health. (Teresa Alvarez)

Teresa's report thesis statement expresses an idea that is accepted by experts and by others who study human health. It is suitable for a report because it does not make a claim that must be proved. Her paper will go on to give specific information about what exactly good nutrition, balanced diet, and exercise involve, and why they are important.

Exercises: Thesis statements

1. Label each of the following according to whatever it expresses: a general topic (GT), a narrowed topic (NT), an argumentative thesis statement (ATS) or a report thesis statement (RTS). (The first two have been done for you.) Be prepared to give reasons for your choices. Start by deciding if it is a grammatically complete sentence (that is, whether it has a full verb and is an independent clause). If it is a complete sentence, then it will be either a report thesis statement (RTS) or an argumentative thesis statement (ATS). If it is not a complete sentence, then it states either a general topic (GT) or a narrowed topic (NT).

ATS 1. Transportation of crude oil in ships is no longer worth the cost.
_NT_ 2. Methods of moving crude oil over land from one part of the world to another.

———— 3. Pipelines are more effective than ships for the transportation of crude oil.

———— 4. Ships as transportation.

———— 5. The French Revolution.

_A_ 6. The use of the guillotine in the French Revolution.

_A_ 7. Although there are difficulties in learning how to use them, certain electronic aids, based on ultrasound or laser beams, must be more widely used to help the blind to become more mobile and independent.

_NT_ 8. Ways in which electronic aids have been used by the blind.

_R_ 9. There are several ways in which electronic aids have been used by the blind.

_R_ 10. Researchers have proposed new ways of helping the blind to move around by means of new electronic aids.

_R_ 11. Television is an important form of entertainment for many people.

_T_ 12. In spite of the fact that freedom of expression is very important, television should be subject to very strict censorship, in order to protect the viewers from bad influences.

_A_ 13. Censorship of television programs is a very bad thing, because it denies full freedom of expression.

_N_ 14. The use of television in education.

_R_ 15. Television is useful in the medical training of first year nursing students.

_A_ 16. All forms of education should be conducted by television, which is more effective than most teachers.

_A_ 17. The humanity, flexibility, and up-to-date information of good teachers can never be replaced by teaching machines, no matter how sophisticated the electronic technology becomes.

_R_ 18. Jogging and swimming are forms of exercise.

_A_ 19. Jogging is better exercise than hatha yoga.

_A_ 20. As a form of exercise, hatha yoga gives results that are different from and superior to those of jogging.

2. The following thesis statements are from student research papers. For each one, first say whether you think the statement is for an argumentative paper or for a report. Then say what kinds of things you think would have to be described or discussed in the paper to ensure a good fit between the paper and its thesis statement.

(a) The property tax of the United States is effective and a major source of income on the local government level, but it will have a reduced role in the future. (Songsan Udomsilp)

R (b) When people retire they have to resolve economic problems, search for new activities, and develop new social roles. (Maria Luisa Morales)

(c) Although many people think that mathematics is closest to physics, astronomy, chemistry, and other sciences, some aspects of musical structure and form are akin to mathematical structures and form. (Kanyanit Luengransun)

(d) Nuclear power technology has taken important steps since the early 1970's and, as a result, a new major source of energy has been developed. (Mostefa Ouki)

A (e) The primary cause of murine muscular dystrophy may be demyelination of nerve fibers. (Maria Moschella)

A (f) Establishing a management information system will help the decision making unit in an organization solve the problems of management. (Yee-Shioung Lin)

☐☰▷ UNIT 8
Preliminary Outline

Assignment

Prepare a preliminary outline of your research paper. Use numbering and indentation to show the different degrees of importance of the headings and subheadings. Hand in the outline to your instructor together with your preliminary thesis statement.

The purpose of the outline is to help you organize your ideas and information. This outline is "preliminary" because it is always the case that writers change their outlines as they discover new information and find better ways to organize it.

The statements of your outline may be written as full sentences or as phrases or single words. It is clearest to use full sentences for the major headings and phrases or words for less important ones. The ideas expressed in major headings are always more general than those of subheadings, which refer to more specific, more detailed aspects of the major headings.

Although this assignment requires you to write a formal outline with numbering and indentation, you may find later, when writing for your academic courses, that a less formal or different type of outline suits you better. (Some writers just list all the points to be mentioned. Others use a "tree" diagram or a "wheel and spokes" diagram to show the relationships between main ideas and supporting ideas.) Whatever approach you use, remember that writing ideas down is not just a way of recording them. It also encourages other ideas and new ways of considering them. It helps you see new connections between familiar things. As with note taking, you can use the writing of a series of rough outlines as a way of exploring and shaping ideas, and not only as a mechanical way of noting what is already formed in your mind.

Examples: Preliminary thesis statement and outline

Two of the following examples have only two levels of numbering and indentation. Another example with three levels, also using Roman numerals, capital letters, and Arabic numerals, can be found in the sample research paper in Unit 14.

How many levels of indentation and numbering there are in an outline depends upon the complexity of the material and the degree to which it has been organized by the writer. The type of numbering system does not matter, but it should be consistent within any one outline.

EXAMPLE 1 (Jose Mugica)

Thesis statement: Predominantly agricultural, the Dominican Republic needs specific information to give impetus to its economic development.

Outline:

   I. There is no possible agricultural development without specific and updated information.
  II. The National Documentation Center for Agriculture must confront the problem.
     A. The status of agricultural information in the Dominican Republic.
     B. The services of the National Documentation Center for Agriculture.
       1. Exchange documents.
       2. Photocopies.
       3. Loan of documents.
       4. Daily Press Bulletin.
       5. Technical consultations.
       6. General summaries.
 III. The main purpose of the National Documentation Center for Agriculture must be fulfilled. It is necessary to improve the Interamerican Agricultural System (AGRINTER).
       1. Providing specific information.
       2. Distributing the information.
       3. Coordinating the National Network for agriculture.
 IV. It is necessary to solve the problem found in the execution of the activities.
     A. The role of the Secretary of Agriculture.
        Timely distribution of resources.
     B. International technical assistance.
       1. Role of the International Institute for Agricultural Cooperation (IICA).
       2. Role of the Food and Agricultural Organization (FAO).

EXAMPLE 2 (Juan Carrasco)

Thesis statement: Man has been developing art for more than forty thousand years because he can only overcome his separateness through the communication and comprehension of his feelings.

Outline:

   I. Artistic language needs to be learned like any other language and perhaps it is one of the hardest to learn.

   A. What is drawing?
   B. Two main categories of drawing.
   C. The graphic elements.
 II. Four factors influence the expressiveness of graphic elements.
   A. The form of perception.
   B. The artist's mind.
   C. Technical media.
   D. Universal symbols.
III. Two drawings can be analyzed to illustrate some of the factors previously summarized.
   A. Line.
   B. Form.
   C. Value and texture.
 IV. Learning artistic language leads to a changed sensibility and receptive attitude.

EXAMPLE 3 (Synian Hwang)

Preliminary Thesis Statement: Statisticians must now consider some spects of the theoretical developments in sampling theorem under the finite population model.

Outline:
   I. Foundations of survey-sampling.
   A. Classical finite population model.
   B. Current finite population model.
  II. An old approach to finite population sampling theory.
   A. Basic model.
   B. The likelihood function.
   C. Best-supported estimates.
   D. The role of randomization.
 III. Sampling theory under certain linear regression models.
   A. Basic model.
   B. Choice of estimator.
   C. Choice of sampling plan.
   D. The role of randomization.
   E. Some empirical results.
 IV. Subjective Bayesian models.
   A. Basic model.
   B. Exchangeable priors.
   C. Results for specific distributions.
  V. Future study.
   A. Missing data.
   B. General model.

⬛▤▷ UNIT 9
Plagiarism

Plagiarism, defined in dictionaries as "stealing and using the ideas or writings of another person as one's own," must be clearly understood and carefully avoided by anyone writing a research paper. Unlike other types of composition in which most of the information comes directly from the writer and is the property of that writer, a research paper must contain great amounts of information and many ideas from the work of others. These other sources must all be acknowledged.

Therefore, it is important that when you are taking notes from sources you should mark carefully on your note cards exactly which words are directly from the source (using quotation marks), which are paraphrase and which are your own.

A complicating factor for some students whose first language is not English is the fact that different cultures may have different attitudes to using others' words and ideas without acknowledgment. In some cultures it may be acceptable because everyone agrees that the words of the original could not be improved. In others, it may be acceptable because the source is considered an authority whose words and ideas are common property as soon as they are published. In yet others it might be regarded as disrespectful and even deceitful to change the words of an original source so they are no longer recognizable. So for practical purposes students from some non-English speaking backgrounds may have to learn to work with a different set of values when using the language and ideas of others in a research paper. These values are based on the idea that it is a serious crime to plagiarize, so serious that in some cases it may lead to a student being expelled from the school.

Follow these guidelines and you will never be guilty of plagiarism:

1. Use your own words and sentence structures when writing your paper, even when writing about the ideas of others.

2. When paraphrasing (putting an idea in your own words), avoid using any words from the original, unless they are essential technical terms.

3. If you use any of the original words from a source, you must acknowledge them by enclosing them in quotation marks. It is still regarded as plagiarism if, without quotation marks, you use some of the original words and phrases from a sentence and change others. Also, it is still regarded as plagiarism if you keep the sentence structure of the original and change all the words to synonyms.

4. Acknowledge all ideas taken from other writers, either in a footnote or as part of the sentence describing the ideas. This applies to any ideas or theories that specialists in the field can recognize as belonging to a specific person. It does not

apply to ideas and information that are common knowledge in the field. This is the most difficult area in which to judge whether something is plagiarised, because over the years ideas which originate with an individual become so generally accepted that their origin is forgotten, and the idea becomes part of the body of knowledge that is central to the subject area and that appears in school textbooks.

Examples

Original text:

> The second problem would have guaranteed the failure of the new math even if the first problem had not existed. The overwhelming majority of elementary-school teachers have had inadequate training in mathematics, and thus did not understand what they were expected to teach. A program that attempts to transmit knowledge not possessed by the teacher is doomed to fail. As this fact became clear to curriculum directors and textbook publishers across the country, they compounded their error by attempting to make the new math teacher-proof. This involved developing self-explanatory materials and mechanical, repetitive techniques which were based on underlying mathematical principles. Unfortunately, the new techniques were far more complicated than the old ones had been, the teachers still didn't understand what was going on, and an entire generation did not learn how to compute. (From: Copperman, P. (1980). *The literacy hoax.* New York: Morrow Quill Paperbacks, p. 65.)

Possible uses of the original text:

EXAMPLE 1

PLAGIARISM: A program that attempts to transmit knowledge not possessed by the teacher is doomed to fail. (This should be in quotation marks.)

NOT PLAGIARISM: ''A program that attempts to transmit knowledge not possessed by the teacher is doomed to fail.'' (The quotation marks make this an acceptable use of the original.)

EXAMPLE 2

PLAGIARISM: A course that attempts to transmit knowledge not possessed by the teacher will never succeed. (This is patchwork plagiarism; a few words are paraphrased, but most are from the original and the sentence structure is also from the original.)

NOT PLAGIARISM: A course ''that attempts to transmit knowledge not possessed by the teacher'' will never succeed. (The quotation marks around words from the original make this acceptable.)

EXAMPLE 3

PLAGIARISM: A course that tries to convey understanding not held by the teacher is fated to be unsuccessful. (This is plagiarism because the original sentence structure has been kept, even though the writer has used synonyms to replace most words.)

NOT PLAGIARISM: If the instructor does not have the knowledge that the student is meant to learn from a course, then the course will never succeed. (This is acceptable because it is a full paraphrase, with original words and sentence structure changed, of an idea that is common knowledge in the field of education.)

EXAMPLE 4

PLAGIARISM: Without the first problem, the second one would still have been enough to stop the new math from working. (Even though this is a full paraphrase, it is plagiarism of the author's idea from the first sentence of the extract, because the idea is not common knowledge in the field of math education.)

NOT PLAGIARISM: Copperman (1980, p. 65) claims that, without the first problem, the second one would still have been enough to stop the new math from working. (This is acceptable because it is a full paraphrase and the author's own idea has been clearly attributed to him.)

NOT PLAGIARISM: Without the first problem, the second one would still have been enough to stop the new math from working (Copperman, 1980, p. 65). (This is acceptable because it is a full paraphrase and the author's own idea has been clearly attributed to him.)

Exercise: Plagiarism

The extract below is followed by some possible uses that could be made of it. For each use, state in one sentence whether or not it is plagiarism and give a reason for your decision. (Plagiarism of ideas, which must usually be judged by an expert in the field, is not included in the exercise.)

Original text:

An even better case can be made that the new English curriculum has directly caused a deterioration in the writing skills of American students. Writing instruction in the early 1960's tended to be rather mechanical. Teachers focused on such aspects of the writing art as grammar, punctuation, syntax, and spelling. This type of instruction was fiercely criticized in the late 1960's as stifling creativity and fostering an imitative kind of writing. In my opinion, some of the criticism was well-founded, especially for bright students, but as usual the baby went out with the bath water. (From: Copperman, P. (1980). *The literacy hoax*. New York: Morrow Quill Paperbacks, p. 100.)

Possible uses of the original text:

1. ". . . the new English curriculum has directly caused a deterioration in the writing skills of American students."

2. Teachers focused on such aspects of the writing art as grammar, punctuation, syntax, and spelling.

3. Instructors concentrated on such parts of the skill of written composition as "grammar, punctuation, syntax, and spelling."

4. A mechanical approach dominated the teaching of composition in the first years of the 1960's.

5. Copperman (1980, p. 100) asserts that some of the criticism of early 1960's writing instruction was justified, especially in the case of intelligent students, and that what was good was thrown out with what was bad: ". . . the baby went out with the bath water."

6. This type of instruction was fiercely criticized in the late 1960's as stifling creativity and fostering an imitative kind of writing.

7. During the later years of the 1960's, two strong criticisms were made of such teaching of writing: first, that the students could not be creative and, second, that only imitative writing was encouraged.

8. One view (Copperman, 1980, p. 100) is that, although there was good evidence to support some of the critical judgements, the effective aspects of instruction were given up together with the ineffective.

 UNIT 10
Note Taking

Assignment

Over a period of a few weeks, make notes for your paper. Write the notes on large file cards. From your set of note cards, select 12 to hand in to your instructor before the due date. These 12 cards should reflect the different kinds of notes that you have taken, so you should hand in:

2 cards that are mainly direct quotations.
5 cards that are summaries using your own words and your own abbreviations.
5 cards that are mainly your own words, but which do not summarize.

In addition to the note itself, on each card write:

A reference to indicate the source (such as author's name, or a letter code previously assigned to each bibliography card).
The page numbers of the pages from which the information was taken.

Add an extra card to the set, with your name and research paper topic written on it (for instructor's information).

Taking notes has three purposes, which are:

(a) to record information so that you do not forget it.
(b) to help you to understand and organize the ideas and information that you get from your reading.
(c) to give you a chance to develop and record your own ideas about your topic, ideas that are stimulated by what you read and by the act of writing.

Even if you are accustomed to taking notes on sheets of paper, not on cards, you should use cards for this assignment, because it will give you the opportunity to try out a different system, one that many people find very efficient. You will save yourself from confusing your notes later in the writing process if you make sure now that each card has a clear indication of which source the note comes from. Each card must also show the exact page numbers that are the origin of the note. The source may be indicated by using the name of the author (for example, write SMITH in one corner for a book or article by John P. Smith). Another way is to give each one of your preliminary bibliography cards a code number or letter; then use that number or letter on your note cards (for example, the book or article by John P. Smith may have a code letter E, in which case each note card from that source will have an E written in one of the corners).

A further technique you can use in order to avoid confusing your cards later (when you are trying out different ways of organizing the information) is to give each a brief heading. One or two words or a short phrase indicating which aspect of your subject is dealt with in each card is enough. Write this heading in one of the corners and place it in parentheses.

The most important thing to remember when taking notes is that you must put quotation marks around *all* words that are not your own (except for technical terms that are common in the subject area). This is because in your paper you must also show clearly which words and ideas are from sources you have read. If you do not show this clearly, you will be guilty of plagiarism.

There are different types of note cards. Some are direct quotations of the author's words; others give the same information, but entirely in the words of the researcher (paraphrase); others summarize (shorten) in either the author's or the researcher's words by choosing only the main ideas; and yet others are combinations of these types. The most common type of note taking is that which summarizes using the writer's own word or phrase abbreviations.

When taking notes you should not rely upon too many direct quotations, because they will form a small part of your final paper (10 percent or less). Sometimes, however, students feel that they should copy down as much as possible (or even photocopy a lot), and they tell themselves that "later" they will try to understand what they have noted (or photocopied). This is a very poor strategy to use, because it leads to a situation in which there is too much to digest at the last minute. Remember that a research paper is a long-term, not a short-term project. You should therefore use the note taking weeks very carefully; this is the time when you develop a real understanding of your topic. It is also the time when you begin to realize what changes must be made in your preliminary thesis and outline. And it is the time when you discover which items to drop from your preliminary bibliography and which new ones to add.

Often writers of research papers get very anxious about the project during the note-taking phase because their ideas and plans keep developing and changing and because they find more references to things that they should read. This is in fact no cause for concern. It is a natural part of writing a long composition that uses sources of information other than your own experience. The aim of research is, after all, to put yourself in a position in which your knowledge and ideas develop and change. You are researching because you want to move from knowing a little about your topic to being an expert on it. So make full use of the activity of note taking as an important way of developing understanding of your subject. Simply writing facts down helps to make you think about the topic and about the connections between different aspects of it.

Examples

Study the examples of note cards of different types on the following pages. They were written by Maite Terrer for her paper on coal as an energy source and Jehad Asfoura for his paper on the link between smoking and cancer.

EXAMPLE 1

Direct quotation and summary with abbreviations (the most common type of note-taking)

```
(cost/demand)
p. 56                                                    D(2)
     "Nevertheless, higher cost marginal coal mines will
only be developed if there is sufficient demand for coal at
prices that will cover costs, and there will only be suffi-
cient demand for coal if coal is a competitive source of
energy."

     Oil will be more expensive in future, so products fr.
coal conv. will compete.  Diff. betw. coal and oil prices
will be lg. enough to allow for high cost of coal conv. and
prodn. of competitive prods.  Rise in oil price cd. affect
demand for coal by increasing prodn. and transp. costs.  But
compet. from coal prods with those frm oil may limit incr.
of oil prices in future.
```

EXAMPLE 2

Summary with abbreviations

```
(coal-based technology)
13-19                                                       C

     Impt. to consider technol. based on coal because of c's
avail. and the possib it cd. subst. for oil as an energy
resource.
     There are technols. capable of using c. to obt. pro-
ducts to subst. for natural oil and gas, e.g. c. gasifica-
tion gives several kinds of products, such as low or medium
BTH gas, wh. can be transformed by other processes into
other gaseous & liquid fuels.
```

EXAMPLE 3

```
(expanded use)
1-10                                                    E
                                                   microfilm

        It is nec. to incr. the prodn. of coal to "provide a
transition" (p. 1) betw. oil and other energy sources.
        "Because of its abundance and versatility (it can be
converted to coke, synthetic gases, liquids and chemical
feedstocks) coal is one of the only alternatives to oil,
natural gas and nuclear power in the near term that can
rapidly increase to meet demands" (p. 3).
        At pres. coal supplies more than 1/4 of world energy,
but will have to supp. betw. 1/2 and 2/3 of the additional
energy needed by the world dur. next 20 yrs. To do so coal
prod. must incr. 2 1/2 to 3 X and world trade in steam coal
must grow 10 to 15 X above 1979 levels. Study's concl. is
simple:  "Without such a coal expansion the world economic
outlook is bleak" (p. 10).
```

Summary, with abbreviations, and some direct quotations

EXAMPLE 4

```
(coal-usage advantages)
65                                                      D


-c. mining industries - employment increase.
 (also in related transportn. industries)
-countries w. no coal will save by purchase of coal inst.
 of oil, for gen. of elec. & other industrial applics.
-subst. by coal will allow the "diversification" of energy
 supplies & reductions in oil-import. dependency
-Utilizn. of coal may incr. the dev. of new technols. wh.
 cd. allow subst. of oil by gas & liquid fuels from coal and
 "higher utilization of the infrastructure for liquid and
 gas fuel distribution."
```

Summary, with abbreviations, and two short direct quotations

EXAMPLE 5

```
(coal production costs)

55-56                                                   D (1)

        Usually t. coal industry has a steady level of cost.
Future:  prices will rise, but less rise than that of oil
prices.
Cost of mining coal cd. be "moderated by increases in labor
productivity" resulting from:

i)    gradual intro. of new mining technologies
ii)   opening of new & more productive c. mines
iii)  expected shift to large-scale surface mining in major
      c. producing countries.

Coal prodn. costs will rise if there is little devpt. of
productive mines.  This will affect c's competitiveness with
alternative energy supplies.
```

Summary, with abbreviations

EXAMPLE 6

Paraphrase and summary

```
(PIPE vs. CIGAR)

p. 43                                                    R

        The incidence of cancer is less among the smokers of
pipes or cigars if we compare them with the cigarette
smokers.  This fact is related to the filtering qualities
of the pipe or the cigar, and the lower consumption of
tobacco among the pipe or cigar smokers.

        The pipe tar is a reason for cancer lesions which cause
the death of mice in 2-3 weeks.
```

EXAMPLE 7

Mainly direct quotation

```
(TYPES OF CANCER)

p. 23                                                    C

        The kinds of cancer which are caused by cigarette smoke
and their sites.

"Cigarette smoke     lung               epidermoid
                     mouth and throat   squamous cell
                     larynx             squamous cell
                     esophagus          squamous cell
                     bladder            transitional"
```

EXAMPLE 8

All direct quotation

```
(EFFECTS OF GIVING UP)

p. 85                                                    F

    "The cessation of smoking reverses the early
pathological changes; as a result, it prevents people from
getting cancer, but it can't reverse the very old changes.
They take several years to extinguish."
```

EXAMPLE 9

```
(TOXINS IN SMOKE)

p. 85                                                     F

     Numerous toxins in cigarette smoke interfere with the
influences of smoking in the organism:  Acrolein, Nitrogen
dioxide, Hydrogen cyanide, Carbon monoxide, but the most
important toxin is Polycyclihydrocarbon "whose possible
carcinogenicity has been receiving increasing attention."
```

Mainly paraphrase, with some direct quotation

EXAMPLE 10

```
(RISK STATISTICS)

p. 309                                                    C

"No. of      No. of    No. of              Relative
cigarettes   cases     controls   Ratio    Risk
    0          3         14       0.21      1.00
   1-9         1          4       0.25      1.77
  10-19        8         16       0.50      2.33
  20-29       24         14       1.71      8.00
  30-39        9          4       2.25     10.50
   40          9          2       4.50     21.00

It demonstrates the relationship of smoking to case-control
status.  There is a direct increase of risk with amount
smoked, using the non-smoker as the reference point
(relative risk = 1)"
```

All direct quotation

EXAMPLE 11

```
(SMOKERS/NON-SMOKERS)
(HEAVY/LIGHT SMOKERS)

p. 7                                                      R

     It has been proved since 1952 in research described to
the American Cancer Society by Dr. Cyder Hammond that
cigarette smokers die from cancer and heart diseases before
non-smokers in the fifty to seventy age range.

     There are many facts about cancer and smoking.  Light
and heavy smoking is associated with an increase of the
death rate, especially from the organs in which cancer
appears, but heavy smoking decides the death rate, and also
there is no difference between the rural or the sub-rural
areas in this problem.
```

Full paraphrase (with no summarizing)

Exercise: Note taking

Select either Extract II or Extract III from the following pages and for that extract write note cards of the following types:

One card   Direct quotation of one or more key sentences. (Use quotation marks.)

One card: Paraphrase of some or all of the final paragraph. (Use your own words with no omission of information and little, if any, direct quotation.)

Two cards: Summary of the whole extract, using your own words and abbreviations.

On each card write the author's name or initials and the page number of the extract, just as you would for your own research paper notes. Extract I has been used as an example.

EXTRACT I

THE CHALLENGE TO INTELLIGENCE TESTING IN SCHOOLS

The usefulness of group intelligence tests in the schools has been severely challenged in recent years. New York City (see *New York Times,* March 31, 1964), Los Angeles (see *Los Angeles Times,* January 31, 1969), and then the State of California have discontinued the use of such tests. Individual intelligence tests given to students needing special attention have continued.

Self-fulfilling Prophecies

This policy of discontinuing IQ testing was defended by Loretan (1965) largely on the basis of the "self-fulfilling prophecy effect" of the IQ measure. As more than one teacher has said, "Once you know the child's IQ, you tend to see him through it, and you adjust your teaching to his ability or level of intelligence—as revealed by the test." In this manner the IQ becomes the basis of a self-fulfilling prophecy to child as well as teacher. The score begins to signify something "given", as if it were a part of the body. Much too often it is used as evidence of what a child is "worth." The effect of this on the initiative of teachers and the self-images of children is appalling to contemplate (Loretan, 1965).

Is the self-fulfilling prophecy powerful enough to influence pupils' IQs? Rosenthal and Jacobson (1968), in a widely publicized book, said yes, but their evidence has been severely discounted in detail by Elashoff and Snow (1971). Nevertheless, effects of teacher expectancy on teacher behavior, pupil behavior in class, and pupil achievement have been found with some consistency in a review of such studies by Baker and Crist (1971).

In place of the group intelligence tests, the New York schools planned to use (a) school grades, (b) achievement tests, and (c) teachers' judgments of intellectual ability. The judgments were to be made with special guides based on the developmental models of Piaget (see Unit 18). These replacements for the intelligence tests would have the advantage, among other things, of yielding measures that would not be attributed to hereditary factors. But it would seem that prophecies about students could occur just as easily from this information as from any other information about a student's level of abilities.

Getting Along Without Intelligence Tests

In responding to the move to ban intelligence testing, Gilbert (1966) noted that instructions to teachers and supervisors had always cautioned against using group intelligence tests with children who are handicapped verbally, culturally, physically, socially, or emotionally. In fact, Gilbert also observed that no textbook of the past 30 years supported the "pure genetic IQ concept." But he admitted that some people acted as if a pure genetic measure of ability were obtained. Thus he regarded the ban as useful if it led to a major educational program on the uses and limitations of intelligence tests and if, when the tests are restored, the term IQ is replaced with a less prejudicial one. (See also Houston, 1964; Yourman, 1964.)

The issue seems to depend on whether what tests of intelligence measure— whether it be called scholastic aptitude, general mental ability, or whatever— can be freed, in the thinking of teachers and parents, of the connotation of unimprovability. Many persons still regard intelligence tests as measuring something fixed—not necessarily hereditary, but certainly beyond the reach of educational influences. This notion seems to be difficult to uproot through popular educational media.

Moreover, when such tests are used as a basis for individualizing instruction, for screening, and for guidance, they tend to put low-income and minority students into the slow, less-enriched classes. The individualization functions can probably be served by other measures—school grades, standardized diagnostic achievement tests, and teachers' judgments—that seem less fixed and can lead to remedial effort.

So getting along without group intelligence tests for at least an experimental period seems worth trying. Intelligence tests may seem less disadvantageous after we try to get along without them. American education is trying to get rid of practices that worsen the disadvantages suffered by students from low-income families and minority-group students. The discontinuation of intelligence testing may serve that purpose. But dropping the tests will serve no purpose if teachers, because of their personal experiences or their prejudices, regard certain groups of students as uneducable. Each student, regardless of group affiliation or test information, is to be helped, from where he is, to some objective. That is the teachers' job.

(Gage, N. L., & Berliner, D. C. [1975]. *Educational psychology.* Chicago: Rand McNally, pp. 233–235.)

The following four note cards from Extract I are examples of what is required in this exercise:

EXAMPLE 1

Direct quotation

> 233   G. and B.
>
>   "In this manner the IQ becomes the basis of a
> self-fulfiling prophecy to child as well as teacher. The
> score begins to signify something 'given', as if it were a
> part of the body."
>
> 234
>
>   "In place of the group intelligence tests, the New York
> schools planned to use (a) school grades, (b) achievement
> tests, and (c) teachers' judgments of intellectual ability.
> The judgments were to be made with special guides based on
> the developmental models of Piaget."

EXAMPLE 2

Full paraphrase
with little
quotation

> 235   G. and B.
>
>   It is a useful experiment to stop using intelligence
> tests for a while, because they may then begin to seem not
> so bad. American education aims to lessen the disadvantages
> of poor and minority students and not having intelligence
> tests may help in this aim. However, not having such tests
> will be no use at all if teachers ("because of their per-
> sonal experiences or their prejudices") think that some
> students are impossible to educate. The teacher's work is
> to help each student to progress from some point to another,
> no matter what group the student is from or what the
> intelligence test score is.

EXAMPLE 3

<table>
<tr><td>

233-5 (cont.)   G. and B.

Gilbert: test instr. give cautions on use of IQ tests and
no textbooks support idea of pure genetic IQ, yet people act
as if the latter were real. So he thinks the ban cd. be
useful.

The issue: can the measure be separated from strong,
popular idea that intell. cannot be improved?

Int. tests work to disadv. of low-income & minority sts.
Other measures (see NY above) not so rigid & can
attempts to improve stn.

Worth trying not to use such tests (wh. may not seem so bad
after a break in using them), but not using will have no
purpose if tchrs still think sm groups uneducable.

</td><td>

**Summary, with ab-
breviations and little
direct quotation**

</td></tr>
</table>

EXAMPLE 3 (Continued)

<table>
<tr><td>

233-5   G. and B.

Intell. tests (exc. for sp. cases) discontinued in NYC, LA
and Ca. because of "self-fulfilling prophecy" effect of I.Q.
(Sts. and trs behave as if IQ shows final value of person
-v. bad for tr. initiative & st. self-image.) Still some
controversy about the effect.

NYC to use, instead, (a) grades (b) achievt. tests (c) tchr.
judgment of intell. (based on Piaget).

Advantage: no heredity in these. Disadvantage: 'prophe-
cies' cd. still occur.

</td><td>

**Continuation of pre-
vious note card**

</td></tr>
</table>

EXTRACT II

GIFTED PUPILS: MANY ARE UNIDENTIFIED, UNDERSERVED

Washington—When she reached 5th grade, Carol, a student from East
Hartford, Conn., was placed in a program for "gifted and talented" students.
Admission to the program was based largely on I.Q. scores; students with
I.Q.'s below 130 were not admitted. Carol, with an I.Q., of 133, was accepted.

But the following year, after Carol's family moved across the river to West
Hartford, her parents learned that in the new district, only students with I.Q.'s
of 135 or higher were classified as "gifted." Hence, Carol would not be able to
take part in the program.

Carol's experience, according to Joseph S. Renzulli, is one of many such cases. It points, he said, to one of the most serious problems in education, for the gifted and talented: defining what "gifted" means and identifying students who meet that definition.

Mr. Renzulli, a psychologist at the University of Connecticut and a pioneer in the field of education for gifted students, was one of several experts on the subject who spoke at a special symposium on "New Directions for Gifted Education" at the annual meeting of the American Psychological Association (A.P.A.), held here last week.

Among the major points of the discussion:

Many bright children are wasting up to half the time they spend in regular classes. And the available data suggest that fewer than half of all gifted students have been identified and placed in special programs attuned to their needs.

Educators too often define a "gifted" child as one who attains exceptionally high scores on tests of academic aptitude and achievement. But, the panelists noted, many children have unusual talents and intangible qualities that are not readily measured on standardized tests.

The special programs that are developed rarely suit the widely varying needs and interests of very bright children.

Measurement and Evaluation

Many of the methods of measurement and evaluation are "characterized by unsophisticated and often inaccurate data collection," said Donald J. Treffinger, an educational psychologist at the State University of New York College at Buffalo. Many districts adopt a "matrix" approach, in which "incomparable data are thrown together" in an effort to create a numerical index of "giftedness." Such indices, he said, defeat the purpose of gathering a wide range of information about the student.

Furthermore, the tests that students take to qualify for a special program may not be an appropriate measure of "giftedness," according to Mr. Treffinger. "There is widespread misuse of tests for purposes for which they were not developed and for which they are not appropriate."

Some school officials rely too heavily on total test scores to establish cutoff points, Mr. Treffinger said. In doing so, he added, they are ignoring the margin of "standard error" that is built into virtually all standardized tests.

The use of standardized tests to identify gifted students is problematic in other ways, Mr. Renzulli said. There are two kinds of giftedness, he believes. The first "schoolhouse giftedness," is found in those students who are "good test takers or lesson learners." The majority of public-school students classified as "gifted" probably fall into this category, Mr. Renzulli said.

But these talents alone offer no guarantee that a student will achieve success.

"History does not remember people who merely learn their lessons well," he said.

The processes of identifying students and developing programs for them should be interrelated, Mr. Treffinger said. Psychological and educational assessments should provide useful information, but test scores alone are not the principal source of such information. "We need a broader profile of students," he said.

The programs themselves, although created with good intentions, are often inadequate, the speakers agreed. Many offer only a few supplemental activities in which all gifted students, regardless of their particular talent, participate.

These programs are premised on the notion that "all gifted students can be treated identically or benefit from a single program," Mr. Treffinger said.

"One of the great paradoxes is that we build programs on the rationale that students have unique talents, then expect the same program to suit them all."

Other speakers, however, questioned whether the public schools have the resources to create effective programs for gifted students.

A recent study by the educational theorist Benjamin S. Bloom found, according to John F. Feldhusen of Purdue University, that many parents with gifted children give up on the public schools and seek special instruction elsewhere. In some cases, school-board policies preclude rapid promotion, and bright students become extremely bored.

Moreover, Mr. Feldhusen said, the gifted are tremendously diverse. "No single program could come close to meeting all their needs. Any notion that we can come up with some single program is unrealistic."

(Walton, S. [1982, September 2]. Gifted pupils: Many are unidentified, underserved. *Education Week*, p. 6.)

EXTRACT III

WHAT KIND OF PLACE IS A UNIVERSITY?

(Herbert A. Simon, Nobel Prizewinner in Economics, delivered the keynote address at the University of Pittsburgh's third annual Honors Convocation, March 14, 1979. Following is part of that address.)

Universities are organizations. An organization theorist who lives in the university is tempted to think about them as an interesting phenomenon—sometimes, after being studied, a very interesting phenomenon indeed. Perhaps the most remarkable thing about universities is how long-lived they are. Few human institutions have had lives as long as individual universities. I'm not speaking just of the university as a type of institution, but of the longevity of the individual universities. The University of Bologna and the University of Paris are about 800 years old, and Oxford and Cambridge are more than 700 years old. And, if my World Almanac is to be trusted, which it usually is, some 16 American Universities celebrated their bicentennials before our nation did.

Now, when an institution is as durable as that—when it lives longer than elephants are reputed to do—it must be flexible. It must be capable of adapting itself to many environments, many social climates, and it must be capable of performing many functions. We can see how this adaptiveness occurs if we look in detail at some of the most durable technologies that the university uses in doing its work. The lecture—something that's happening right now—the lecture is one of those durable technologies. The lecture, in those ancient universities, was instituted before the invention of printing; and it was terribly essential then. It provided a way of transmitting and copying knowledge. And yet the lecture survived the invention of printing in the 15th century. I try to persuade my students, when they are busy taking notes, that printing does it much faster and cheaper, that perhaps they had better just sit and listen and let their pens be quiet for a while.

The lecture has even survived the invention of TV. And I think it will continue to survive because, in addition to its overt function of transmitting knowledge, such knowledge as can be discovered in the words of the lecturer, it fulfills many implicit functions: implicit functions for the teacher and implicit functions for the students in the lecture room. For the teacher who is a little bit of an actor and a ham (not all actors are hams, you understand, nor are all teachers who are actors hams): but to put it more objectively, for a teacher who enjoys interaction with an audience, the lecture room is a fine place to experience those pleasures and exercise those skills. For the shy teacher who is earnestly enthusiastic about his subject, but who finds intimate contact with other human beings sometimes a little difficult, there is immediately behind him the blackboard, and he can resolutely turn his face to it, impart his knowledge to the blackboard, and have it reflected to the audience.

The student can be an eager participant in the lecture room with his hand frantically waving to gain the attention of the teacher. Or the student can listen and earnestly absorb; he can practice his skills of penmanship; he can sit quietly in his seat and dream his dreams. It's because of the flexibility of that social setting, because not all of us have to be doing the same thing, thinking the same thing, acting the same way, that I think the lecture has survived even at a time when, from a superficial standpoint, we would have thought that it had lost its central and original function to the printing press and to other methods of transmitting knowledge.

Now we can take the lesson and apply it to the university as a whole. The university, too, has many functions. Professors think of the university as a place where new knowledge is created and old knowledge is reinterpreted. With students, you have to determine which students you're talking about before you can say what the function of the university is for them. For some students it's a place where knowledge is transmitted to them because they want to become professors, or they want to prepare themselves for professions, or some other kind of useful livelihood. For others, quite apart from the formal transmission of knowledge, they think that it is a good environment in which to grow to adulthood, or to find a wife or a husband, or to make useful friends—or just friends, useful or not—or to taste of liberal education. All these and more are the motives that bring students to universities, and not all of the motives apply to all students.

The marvel about it is that these functions co-exist, usually amiably, but almost always fruitfully on the campus. Nor is it necessary that a university be just one of these things or serve just one of these functions even for a single student. In particular, the conflict often announced between professional and liberal goals of education is largely illusory. Professional subjects can and should be taught in a liberal way. And liberal subjects can and should be taught with due regard and attention for their usefulness in what we in the universities call the "Real World," the world that the students are going to enter when they leave the university halls.

Today we celebrate the role of the university in the transmission and especially in the creation of knowledge. And we do so on a singularly appropriate date, the 100th anniversary of Albert Einstein's birth. The role, the creation of knowledge, is the university's essential role, without which the others are vain and empty. I'm sometimes rather amazed at how little this is understood outside the university, by the public, sometimes even by university trustees.

(Simon, H. A. [1981]. What kind of place is a university? *The Pittsburgh Undergraduate Review, 2,* 104–110.)

Revised Thesis Statement

Assignment

Revise your thesis statement on the basis of the new ideas and insights you have developed during note taking. Write down the following:

(a) Your preliminary thesis statement (one sentence).
(b) Your revised thesis statement (one sentence).
(c) One or two sentences explaining why you have changed your thesis statement from (a) to (b).

Hand this in to your instructor by the due date. If you have made more than one revision in your thesis statement, write down the intermediate revisions under (b), labeling them "First revision," "Second revision," and so on. If you have made no changes at all in your preliminary thesis statement, write it down in its original form and add next to it in parentheses: "No change."

Your preliminary thesis statement is not likely to remain unchanged. It was formulated at a stage in the research paper process when you knew much less than you do now. On the basis of preliminary reading, you came up with a thesis that you felt would possibly express your main conclusion. This thesis was a guide and focus for your reading.

Now that you have done most of your reading and note taking, you are in a position to know how you will have to change your preliminary thesis statement.

Many researchers find that they can narrow it down even more than they originally thought. Others refine the statement in small ways. Some even decide that their statement should be making a claim opposite to the one they started with.

Such changes and developments are part of the flow of research, not indications of an inability to think clearly and consistently. The purpose of your work is to find out what you can, in the case of an argumentative research paper. So you must expect to modify and change your ideas, even the central thesis, as you move from knowing little to knowing a lot.

The thesis statement of a report, in contrast to that of an argumentative paper, is not likely to be changed in any major ways, except that it will probably be narrowed down more.

⬛⬛➤ UNIT 12
Revised Outline

Assignment

Revise your outline on the basis of the new ideas you have developed during note taking. Again use numbers, letters and indentation to show the relative importance and relationship of ideas. Hand in the revised outline by the due date. Also hand in the preliminary outline.

The outline that you prepare at this stage should be more detailed than the preliminary one. However, it still remains a guide and not something that you should feel trapped by.

After all the reading and note taking that you have now done, there should be a clearer framework of thoughts in your mind for the overall structure of the paper—that is, for how the main sections will connect with your thesis statement, and how the subsections will tie in with the main sections.

Writing an outline in this way and revising it helps you to discover ways of organizing your information. It is not the same thing as turning over in your mind the different possibilities without ever writing them down. Seeing ideas in written form on the paper gives you a different kind of opportunity to change them and reorganize them. The numbers, letters, and indentation are clear indications of how ideas relate to each other. You can "play" with these to find different, perhaps better, ways to sort things out.

Whatever outline you produce now, remember that it can still be changed. The process of producing your research is an ongoing one, with potential for change and improvement at all stages before the final date.

 UNIT 13
Sample Draft

Assignment

Write a draft of part of your research paper, using your note cards as a basis. This sample draft should be no longer than two pages (double-spaced typing or equivalent). It must not include the introduction or conclusion of the paper; instead, it must be an extract from the body of the paper. *Hand in the relevant note cards together with the written assignment.* Although this is a draft, it should be written neatly and legibly. Do not include citations or bibliography in this two-page sample draft.

Many writers of research papers begin to worry most of all at this point in the activity, but this only happens if they misunderstand what they have to do. They do not have to produce perfect sentences, one after another, building up into perfectly good paragraphs that become a good final product, all in the first rough draft. Skilled and experienced writers do not normally work this way (though a few, very rare ones do manage to do most of the writing and rewriting in their minds before beginning the initial draft). The normal procedure, which you should learn to feel comfortable with, by practicing it now, is this:

Select the part of the paper that you want to work on.

Read, reread, and reread the note cards relevant to that section.

Begin to write what you think might possibly be a relevant set of ideas. Do not imagine that you must write logically, coherently, and correctly at this point.

Have only one aim as you start on the draft: to let the ideas come out onto the page. No one except you will see what you are writing now, so do not let your notions of correctness and coherence take control.

When you run out of ideas, go back to your note cards and read them again. Use them to stimulate a fresh flow of thoughts. Write these down as they come to you.

When you run out of ideas again and your notes give you no further help, the natural state of affairs, even for professional writers, you can begin to work on some other part of your paper or reread what you have written so far. (If this does not help, you probably need a break from the work!)

If you choose to go over what you have written so far, you can now begin to change the order of ideas, omit some ideas, or add new ones; you can now cross out, add to, or change any of the words, phrases, clauses, or sentences. Or, as some people do, you may just study what you have drafted as a preliminary to writing another rough draft.

You may decide to produce several rough drafts for this assignment. Or you may produce only one. Whatever the case, it is only while writing the draft which you will hand in to your instructor that you should be concerned with small details of grammar, spelling, and punctuation.

Remember: the seemingly messy and disorganized stages of writing drafts are an ordinary and perfectly natural part of composing. Not only are they natural and ordinary, they are really essential. After all, before you can begin to organize a mixed bag of ideas, you must spread them out before yourself. Often, you will not even have an exact idea of the contents of the bag before you spread the bits and pieces out. And when you first look at what comes out, you may think that it is all too chaotic and disorganized to make sense of. But, if you study it for long enough, you will begin to make sense of it. You will begin to see relationships between the parts. Seeing these relationships is the first element in composing a draft.

The process described here is the same for all writers, but, often, ESL students, feeling helpless and frustrated at the thought of a research paper to be written, imagine that their difficulties are all due to language use. In fact native speakers of English (including experienced writers) often feel the same way. Writing frequently involves periods of feeling "blank," "dry," or "without ideas." This feeling which writers quite often suffer from—that they cannot continue, that they have nothing to say—is usually called "writer's block." It is a terrible sensation, but it passes! You can sometimes help it pass by just taking a break or working on some other task or a different part of the paper.

Finally, remember that a long research paper, just like published books and articles, is the outcome of many drafts and much revising. Your paper will be written in bits and pieces over a period of many weeks, and the order in which you work on these parts is not likely to be their order in the final draft. Never expect to write such a paper straight through from beginning to end, even if you have excellent note cards.

Example of rough draft

The part of a rough draft shown below is one of the drafts (not the final one) written for the explanation of this unit. It is an example of one stage that one writer went through before arriving at a draft that could be given to someone else to read. It is very likely that you will go through some similar drafting stage to produce the sample draft called for in this section and, later, to produce the other parts of your research paper. (*Note:* The *sample* draft to be handed in to your instructor, required for this unit, should *not* look like this *rough* draft; the sample draft is a revised, neater version of a preliminary rough draft.)

Marking the pages of a draft as in this example is not the only way to reorganize the parts of a rough draft.

Many writers rearrange the sections of a draft by means of a "cut and paste" method. That is, they use scissors to cut up the pages of the draft into segments; these segments are then moved about and pasted, or otherwise stuck, in their new position. You should experiment with the cut and paste method to see if it suits your purpose.

go back over this and change *as necessary* the order of ideas, cross out parts, insert new ~~ideas~~ words, phrases and sentences, ~~and so on.~~ Remember that ~~the~~ *a* final draft of good writing has always *first* gone through the *is seemingly* messy, apparently disorganized stage. No one ever produces a ~~polished research pap~~ good piece of expository writing without going through the ~~initial stages~~ phases of apparent chaos. It is *sometimes worrying* quite ~~distressing~~ to in-experienced ~~writing~~ writers to see that they cannot write ~~excellently~~ perfectly grammatical sentences and perfectly coherent compositions on the very first draft. Sometimes this worry *even* prevents them from trying to start. Their anxiety is not necessary. Too much of this type of anxiety is a hindrance not a help, though a small amount of it, a little adrenalin, is sometimes thought to be helpful. The books and articles they see published are all the outcome of much drafting and

PAR

to end

◼◼▷ UNIT 14
Preliminary Draft

Assignment

Prepare a draft of your research paper, consisting of the following parts:

Cover page
Thesis statement and outline
Text of the paper (including reference citations)
Bibliography

Although this is not the final version of your paper, it should be written in clear handwriting or typed. Hand it in by the due date. (Refer to Units 16 and 17 for examples of format.)

The aim of writing this preliminary draft is to make an attempt to pull all the parts of your paper together. The text of the paper is what will occupy you most of all at this stage. This is where you draft and redraft sections of the paper. It is where you organize and reorganize words, phrases, clauses, sentences, paragraphs, and larger units. Other than writing the text of your paper, the requirements of this assignment are mechanical. They are concerned with layout and acknowledgments of sources. (Units 16 and 17 give information about and examples of different formats.)

The parts of this assignment are the same as those you will be asked for in the final assignment. They are requested here in order to give your instructor an opportunity to help you with all aspects of the paper—from small points of grammar and format to larger issues of overall organization and coherence.

If you do not follow the format and documentation style of the model research papers (Units 16 and 17), then you must submit with your draft one or two photocopied pages from a published example of the style you are following.

COVER PAGE

This has no purpose other than to give your work an efficient and neat look and to help your instructor (whose desk may be a muddle of papers from several courses) keep track of all the papers he or she must deal with. Write the *title* of your paper in the center of the page. Below that, write *your name*, your *class or course number*, the *instructor's name*, and the *date*.

TITLE

The title should be a brief indication of the content of the paper. It should not be too long (and should not be a complete sentence). At the same time it should not be so short that it is too vague and general.

THESIS STATEMENT AND OUTLINE

Although your instructor has already seen your preliminary and revised outlines, they are included here because you can revise them again. Also, when reading your paper, your instructor can use your thesis statement and outline as a guide to understanding the intended structure of your paper. Inclusion of these is not, however, a requirement in all papers for academic courses (In a paper for publication, an abstract (summary) replaces the thesis statement and outline.)

TEXT OF THE PAPER

As stated above, this is the part that you spend most time on. This is what most people refer to as "composing a paper"—writing many pages of coherent text. In fact, the process of composing started as soon as you were given the task and began your search for a topic.

So even before you settle on an idea or topic for the paper, you have begun composing. By now, you have already done a great amount of work towards the paper: narrowing the subject, reading for a preliminary bibliography, preparing preliminary and revised versions of your thesis statement and outline, taking notes, and writing a sample draft of part of the paper. So do not think of this as the beginning of the "real" task of writing the paper. Writing a paper consists of getting ideas, playing with them, refining them, reading about the subject, note taking—all of this is part of the process. As you write this preliminary draft, think of it as a try-out of how a certain set of ideas and sentences will look on the page; imagine that you are playing with ways of putting together all that you know. This is not the final draft, so do not inhibit yourself by believing that it should all come out completely coherently and well polished. It should of course be legible and neat; your instructor cannot help you if the draft is difficult to read.

The draft you hand in may not be the very first one you write. Most writers agree that in writing the first draft they are somehow discovering what they want to say. That is, what comes out in this draft will be something that the writer of the paper may use only as a starting point. It is a way of seeing, all in one place, what is available. And the way it comes out is one way of organizing it. As the writer looks over the very first draft, other ways of organizing it may occur to him or her, new ideas about the content may come to mind; new refinements of the thesis statement may come about. All this can be included in the later drafts, one of which can be the preliminary draft turned in to the instructor.

In composing the text of the paper, do not let yourself get stuck on any one part—whether the introduction or any other. If you find you are not making progress on one section, move on to another. Research papers are not written in one, single beginning-to-end flow. Work on different parts, using your outline as a guide, to avoid the frustration of feeling you are at a dead end.

When you have written enough on each separate section of the paper to put together a reasonable preliminary draft, give careful thought to transitions between the sections. Between major sections, you will often need a complete, but short, paragraph of which the only function is to provide the transition. Between paragraphs within one major section, you will usually need a transitional sentence at the end of the first or the beginning of the next. Between sentences, you will often need transitional words or phrases, repetition of key words, or reference words (such as pronouns and demonstratives) to create cohesion.

ORGANIZATION OF IDEAS AND INFORMATION

There are many ways of organizing information in a research paper. The ways you choose will be determined by your purpose. In many college courses in composition the following are taught as the basic "rhetorical patterns":

Chronological order (time order: first to last, or last to first).
Spatial arrangement (physical location of parts).
Comparison (similarities and differences).
Analogy (comparison emphasizing similarities).
Contrast (differences).
Increasing importance (least to most important).
Decreasing importance (most to least important).
Decreasing generality (general to specific).
Increasing generality (specific to general).
Development by examples (using examples to support explanations).
Cause and effect (what happens, with reasons why it happens).
Definition (stating the group to which something belongs and how it is different
    from other members of the same group).
Classification (grouping things together in a logical way).
Logical Division (analysis into parts).

Very few compositions can use only one of these. Most compositions, especially research papers, make use of a combination of various patterns and it is usually impossible to make neat separations between them in any one paper.

For most writers it is not very useful to think too much about the exact pattern that is to be used. So, when writing your paper, think, instead, of the idea that is to be conveyed and try to find the words for that idea. When this is done and you look back over what you have written, you will find that it probably falls quite naturally and without deliberate planning into the appropriate patterns. Occasionally, however, thinking consciously about the rhetorical patterns can help to clarify what you want to say.

INTRODUCTIONS

Write the introduction to your paper last, so that you can make it a guide to the content and structure of the paper. Remember that you will discover things to say or add or change as you write the first drafts, so it would be a waste of time to prepare a polished introduction first. By not writing the introduction at the very beginning, you do not feel trapped by it and your paper will develop more easily.

The first part of your introduction should state the general context of your topic, usually with some reference to work done by others. Then you should indicate what your paper will focus on: your thesis statement comes in at this point. In the last part of your introduction you can help the reader greatly if you give a very brief summary of the main points you will cover. That is, the main points of your outline can be mentioned here (of course, in the form of a few consecutive sentences, not in the indented and numbered format).

CONCLUSIONS

A good conclusion to a research paper is the logical outcome of all that has been said earlier. Usually, the thesis statement is repeated, but not in exactly the same wording. Sometimes certain actions or further research are recommended in a conclusion. And occasionally a research paper ends with an effective quotation. When writing the conclusion to your paper, you should normally aim not to end too suddenly, too abruptly. So it is useful to restate the main points of your paper in a very summarized form and in different words, before restating the controlling idea.

USING QUOTATIONS

Although direct quotations appear in most research papers, they are not usually an important part of them. Some papers make very little use of them. Reference to the work of others is central to research papers, but most of the reference is in the form of indirect speech. You should use direct quotations only when they are very relevant, when they express something in a very special or effective way or when they are good examples of ideas that you will focus on. As a general guideline, try to keep direct quotations at well below ten percent of your whole paper. Your instructor is, after all, interested in how *you* express yourself and not in the words of others.

Take care to weave direct quotations smoothly into the text of your paper by using suitable introductory phrases and expressions. (See Unit 16 for examples and format of long and short quotations.)

THE READER

As you write you will constantly be making decisions about what to put into the paper and what to leave out. The choice is determined by who will read what you write. Although you will be handing your paper in to one instructor, you should not think of that individual as the audience or reader of your paper. A research paper is written for an audience that is knowledgeable in the subject. You should think of the instructor as being typical of such an audience, but do not try to work out what this individual instructor knows about your topic. Instead, from your reading of books and articles, you will get an understanding of what is common knowledge in the field and what is specialized. Think of your readers as having a good general knowledge of the subject and some knowledge about your narrowed topic. Think of yourself as the expert in the very specific focus of your thesis statement. In this way you will not include information that is well known to your readers and you will not leave out what is needed for them to follow your discussion. This is especially important in argumentative papers. In writing a report you can avoid telling your readers what they already know by emphasizing up-to-date ideas and information, for example from recent journal articles (not from standard textbooks or encyclopedias, which include what the audience should know quite well).

 **UNIT 15**
Final Draft

Assignment

Write the final draft of your research paper, including in it any corrections and revisions suggested by your instructor. Also include any further revisions and improvements that you think are necessary. The final draft, like the preliminary draft, should consist of:

Cover page
Thesis statement and outline
Text of the paper (including reference citations)
Bibliography

This draft must be neatly handwritten or typed, with few, if any, obvious erasures or crossings out. Hand it in by the due date, together with the copy of the preliminary draft on which your instructor wrote comments.

The final draft of a research paper for an academic course is the end result of a long process. In theory, it is always possible to make the process continue indefinitely, because no piece of writing is ever really complete; it could always be improved in some way. But the practical limitations of having to write a paper in only one term make it necessary for the writer to compromise. There is no time to continue rewriting. So at this stage try to be satisfied with what you have.

Write out the final draft as neatly as possible. Then edit it for mechanical errors—spelling, grammar, paragraphing, and punctuation.

To reach this stage of your paper, editing a final draft, you have had to work through many different assignments in this book, starting with the initial searching for an idea. Each step is something you have had to think about carefully and do deliberately, with assistance from your instructor in many phases. As you get more practice in writing such papers, you will not have to take each step so deliberately. The stages of this complex process will become habitual and will flow into each other.

In your academic courses, when you turn in the final draft, your instructor will assume that all the steps have been taken, since without them a good paper cannot be produced. In most academic courses, the final draft is the only thing that the instructor sees. In a few courses, however, there may be some guidance, especially in the selection and limitation of a topic. A preliminary thesis statement and outline may be asked for by the instructor; or, this may take the form of a statement of the "problem" (the narrowed topic) and its "rationale" (the reason for investigating this topic). Very rarely is any further help routinely given to all students in the class, but instructors are generally willing to discuss individual research problems as they arise. In many colleges it is also possible to get help with writing problems from departments variously referred to as "Writing Workshop," "Writing Center," "Writing Lab," "Study Skills Center," and so on. Do not hesitate to approach such centers (which normally provide their help at no charge). The experienced tutors there have come across most kinds of research and writing difficulty and will be able to help you.

Your best help, however, will come from going through the research paper composing process several times in the manner suggested by this guide: think initially of the aim of the whole paper and then break down the process of completing it into a series of manageable stages, corresponding to the sequence of assignments given here. In this way you are less likely to find the process overwhelming. It may remain difficult, because writing in any langue, native or foreign, is usually difficult and demanding, but you will be confident that your difficulties and problems are part of the process for everyone and not yours alone. Overcoming these research and writing difficulties, learning about your topic and becoming an expert in it, and completing the research paper task are the personal satisfactions to be gained from seeing the process through from beginning to end.

◧▦▷ UNIT 16
Format of a Research Paper in APA Editorial Style

Providing reference citations and a bibliography is often referred to as "document-ing your sources." The purpose of this is to allow your readers, if they so wish, to find the documents you have used. They may want to do this because of interest in the topic or because they want to check on how you have made use of the source. A second reason for documenting is to make full acknowledgment of the sources you have used. This reason is tied to the question of plagiarism. You do not want your readers to think that you have been stealing ideas. Any ideas that you use that are not your own must be acknowledged, just as you must acknowledge any phrases, sentences, or special uses of words that you get from your sources. Ideas or terms that have become widely current in a field, to the extent that it would be impossible to track down the "owner" or originator of them, do not need to be acknowledged.

There are different ways of citing references according to different style guides and different disciplines. The one used in this book is the increasingly popular author/date system. In this system, the citations are given in parentheses im-mediately following the information to be acknowledged. The reader can then refer to the reference list for the publication and title details. In other systems, citations are given as footnotes at the bottom of each page or as footnotes on a separate page at the end of the paper. (When they are on a separate page at the end may also be referred to as "endnotes" or simply "notes"). In all systems a reference list is given listing all the sources referred to in the paper.

The information given below, adapted from the APA manual is adequate for most student papers. It is not, however, complete. For further detail, consult the manual itself.

QUOTATIONS

Short quotations (up to four lines) are made part of the text and are enclosed in double quotation marks.

Longer quotations are indented five spaces as a block, with no quotation marks. Continue to double space lines in a block quotation.

For all quotations, cite author, year, and page number(s). In parentheses include information not mentioned in the text; for instance, if the author's name is in the text, there is no need to repeat it in parentheses.

Three ellipsis points (. . .) indicate words omitted from within a sentence. Four ellipsis points show omission of words between sentences.

Use square brackets to enclose material that is not part of the original quotation.

Within double quotation marks, use single quotation marks for quoted material or words that would otherwise be in double quotation marks. Within a block quotation use double quotation marks.

Here are three examples:

Quotation 1.　She comments, "The test results are 'contaminated' . . . because of influence from the way it was administered" (Lee, 1984, p. 63).

Quotation 2.　According to Lee (1984), "the test results are 'contaminated' " (p. 63) due to faulty administrative procedures.

Quotation 3.　Lee (1984) makes the following comments about the tests:

> The experimenters allowed them [the candidates] to work with all the questions before the day of the experiment. They should have allowed half of the candidates to work with the first set of questions, and the other half to work with the second set. The test results are "contaminated" . . . because of influence from the way it was administered (p. 63).

REFERENCE CITATIONS

Cite the author's last name, the year of publication and, whenever possible, the page numbers. Place in parentheses what is not mentioned in the text, as in these examples:

> Lee (1981) states that . . .
> It has recently been claimed (Lee, 1979) that . . .

Sometimes both year and date are in the text, so nothing is added in parentheses:

> In 1968, Lee denied that . . .

With page numbers the above examples would appear like this:

> Lee (1981, p. 76) states that . . .
> It has recently been claimed (Lee, 1979, pp. 22–24) that . . .
> In 1968, Lee (pp. 201–202) denied that . . .

When there are two authors, give both names every time they are cited.

Where there are more than two authors, give all the authors' names when they are first cited; thereafter, give only the first author's name and ad "et al." For example, a first citation might be:

> Gonzalez, al-Ali, Chang and Jones (1966) noted that . . .

and a later citation of the same work would be:

> Gonzalez et al, also noted that . . .

and others.

When one author has published more than one work in the same year, add the letters a, b, c, etc., to the year in the reference citation and to the year in the listing of these items in the references:

Peterson (1982b, p. 602) explains the . . .

When citing something indirectly, follow one of these examples:

Jones (1928, p. 26) quotes Smith as saying . . .
Smith (quoted by Jones, 1928, p. 26) states . . .
Smith is cited by Jones (1928, p. 26) as stating . . .

BIBLIOGRAPHY/REFERENCES

The APA manual recommends that the term ''references'' be used for works that directly support a paper and that the term ''bibliography'' be used for a list including background or further reading. So, if you use the heading ''references,'' everything in the list must be mentioned somewhere in the text and everything mentioned in the text must appear in the list. If you use the heading ''bibliography,'' you may add to the list some items that are not directly referred to in the text.

For the format of entries in a bibliography, refer to the earlier section on preparing a preliminary bibliography. In addition: alphabetize the entries, but do not number them; double space between lines; start the first line of each entry at the margin; indent additional lines of each entry (three spaces indentation if typing).

FOOTNOTES

Footnotes may explain or amplify material in the text, but they are distracting to a reader. Whenever possible this information should be made part of the text. When used, they appear after the reference list. Such footnotes are numbered and are referred to in the text by a raised number, for example:

would further the development of ideas[22] and . . .

TABLES

Use tables if they help to make the written information clearer, without just repeating that information. The table number and heading are placed at the top left of the table. Here is an example:

Table 12
Number of Correct Selections Made by Each Color Group

Experiment	Color Group			
	Red	Green	Blue	Yellow
1	26	22	31	19
2	25	42	30	28
3	13	16	33	12

Tables should be included in the text of the paper. For student papers, it is more convenient to place the table on a separate page in the text, which should be included in the page numbering of the paper.

FIGURES

In APA style, the term "figure" is used for any illustration other than a table. (Figures cannot be typed; tables can be typed.)

Use figures only if they help to support the text. As with tables, include them in the text, but, for convenience in a student paper, place them on a separate, numbered page. The figure number and caption are placed at the bottom of the graph or illustration, as in this example:

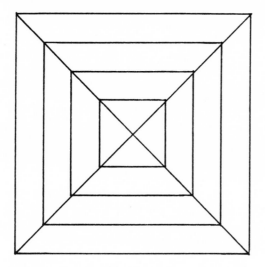

Figure 3. Perceptual variation: Does this represent a view looking down onto a solid object with steps on the outside, or a view looking into a hollow object with steps on the inside?

PAGE NUMBERING

Use Arabic numerals in the top right-hand corner for page numbering. Start counting with the cover page, but do not write the page number on it. The numbers are written on all other pages, including the first page of the text.

HEADINGS AND SUBHEADINGS IN THE TEXT

In a student paper it is usually not necessary to use headings and subheadings in the text, though in some technical and scientific papers they are frequently used.

Such headings must *not* be a substitute for transitional sentences and paragraphs. Use them *only* if they are a definite requirement in papers in your subject area. In a short paper, headings such as ''Introduction'' and ''Conclusion'' are a waste of time; it is taken for granted that the first few paragraphs are introductory and that the last few are the conclusion. If you use headings in the text, center and underline them thus:

<u>A Centered Heading</u>

Sample Research Paper

The sample paper on the next pages follows the style of the *Publication Manual of the American Psychological Association*. Comments have been placed at appropriate places in the right-hand margin to draw attention to various aspects of format and style. Only first and last pages of the sample paper are presented here; the middle pages are omitted. Use 8½ x 11 inch sheets of paper throughout. (The sample papers reproduced in this book are printed in a smaller space only to provide a margin for explanatory comments.)

Staff Communication in an

Academic Library

Chen-Chu Kao

Linguistics 9
Instructor: Sue Hershelman
April, 1984

The cover page con-
tains: title, author,
course number, in-
structor's name,
date.

Capitalize the initial
letters of important
words (not articles
and prepositions) in
the title.

Center the title on
the page.

If the title is more
than one line, double
space between lines.

Place the author's
name, centered, a
few lines below the
title.

Place the remaining
information, also
centered, lower on
the page.

This cover page is
counted in page
numbering, but the
number is not writ-
ten on the page.

Start page numbers in the top right-hand corner.

2

Repeat the title at the beginning of the thesis statement and outline page(s).

Staff Communication in an

Academic Library

Thesis statement

Write the thesis statement at the top of the page, after the subheading: *Thesis statement*.

Effective communication within the library is vital to administration, so improvement of communication should be seen as a contribution to staff morale and library service.

Write the outline below the thesis statement, after the subheading: *Outline*.

Outline

I.   Administration and communication, in general and in an academic library.

II. The nature of and the problems in communication should be recognized.

In the outline, indicate the comparative importance of different parts by using indentation, together with Roman numerals, capital letters, and Arabic numerals.

A.   The emphasis on interpersonal relations theories in management.

B.   The functions of communication.

1.   To transmit information.

2.   To persuade.

3.   To initiate an action.

4.   To facilitate social contact.

C.   The barriers to communication.

1.   Threat to ego.

2.   Ambiguity.

Leave a margin on the left of all handwritten pages. (When typing leave margins of 1-1½ inches at the left, right, top and bottom.)

D.   The gateways to communication.

1.   Attention.

2.   Feedback.

3

III. Messages flow through formal and informal channels of communication.

Write only on one side of each sheet.

    A. Formal communication must be three-directional.

        1. Downward communication.

        2. Upward communication.

        3. Horizontal communication.

    B. Informal communication arises from the social relationships of people.

IV. Messages are diffused by spoken and written communication.

    A. The forms of spoken communication.

        1. The technique of listening.

        2. Face-to-face discussion.

        3. Staff meetings.

        4. Employment interviews.

        5. Telephone conversations.

    B. The forms of written communication.

        1. Staff handbooks and manuals.

        2. Memoranda and reports.

        3. News sheets and magazines.

        4. Noticeboards.

V. Communication, morale and democracy are inter-related within the library.

    A. Communication increases staff morale.

        1. Staff loyalty.

        2. Cooperation.

    B. Communication improves library service.

4

Staff Communication in an

Academic Libary

**Write title at begin-
ning of first page of
text. Leave a space
of a few lines be-
tween the title and
the first paragraph.**

**Double space be-
tween all lines of the
text.**

**Indent the first and
subsequent para-
graphs (when typing,
indent five spaces).
In this sample paper,
the first two para-
graphs are the intro-
duction.**

**Quotation: when au-
thors' names are
mentioned in the
text, only the date
and page number
are given in par-
entheses.**

**The thesis statement
appears at the end of
the introduction (last
sentence of second
paragraph).**

Communication with others is an integral part of our social
life. Without communication there is no organization, for there
is no possibility of the group influencing individual behavior. We
should be aware that the need for internal communication cannot be
neglected by administration. As Rogers and Weber state, "organizational complexity and fragmentation, geographical dispersion,
and particularly the number of levels from lowest to highest,
intensify the need for communication" (1971, p. 82). Therefore,
communication is the keystone of good administration.

In an academic library, staff communication becomes an important aspect of everyday activities. Even though many librarians
assume that their communicative activities are adequate, they
should make more efforts to consider and evaluate communication
among staff. Nowadays, we still find problems arising from inadequate communication which negatively influences staff morale and
group performance. We should realize that effective communication
within the library is vital to administration, and so improvement
of communication should be seen as a contribution to staff morale
and library service.

It is only recently that the emphasis on communication has
emerged in management literature. Certain new theories are characterized by the growing involvement of people in organizational
decision-making. One of the new theories is the human relations
school which is based on psychology and sociology. This school is
primarily concerned with the study of people as human beings.

5

Stueart and Eastlick (1977, p. 21) emphasize that the theme of   **Citation**
this school is that management study should center on interper-
sonal relations. As a result, personnel administration becomes
important, and increasing efforts toward better understanding of
group behavior are evident. Closely related to the human relations school, the social system school encourages employee participation in on-the-job social groups and in decision-making.
The study of this school reveals that communication is the first
function of management and interpersonal communication yields
positive effects in morale (Stueart and Eastlick, 1977, p. 22).   **Citation**

These two theories seem especially suitable to an academic
library, which is made up of intellectual and rational people. As
we know, many staff members in such a library possess advanced
degrees and are demanding more organizational agreement to their
participation. To achieve staff democratic purposes and to pro-
mote high morale, the administration must recognize the importance
of communication as essential to the welfare of the library.

Before identifying the functions of communication, we should
clarify the notion of communication. Beach defines it as "the
transfer of information and understanding from person to person"   **Quotation, with cita-**
                                                                     tion
(1975, p. 583). It is an exchange of meaning so that one individual or group receives information and understanding from other
individuals or groups. In other words, communication is a two-way
process. The interchange of thought must bring out mutual understanding, confidence and good human relations.

As stated above, communication answers not only "what" but   **This short paragraph**
                                                                    is transitional.
also "why." The "what" is the information transmitted, and the

6

"why" is the understanding received. Usually such communication

Citation

serves four functions (Beach, 1975, pp. 580-581).

**Transition words
such as "first" and
"second" help the
reader to understand
how the information
is organized.**

First, communication serves to disseminate information. In

preparing to communicate, the sender must collect all the facts

necessary for his message and choose the proper method to achieve

his purpose in transmitting information. For example the

librarian may inform staff of developments resulting from deci-

sions already taken. The staff receive information necessary for

them to handle their jobs.

Second, communication helps to mold attitude in order to con-

vince and so influence behavior. For instance, the library

superior discusses a problem with his staff and invites ideas for

its solution. He tells the staff how they are getting along and

what changes will influence their work. As a matter of fact, the

superior and staff are influenced by the change of

The middle pages of this sample paper have been omitted.

Citation

(Emery, 1975, p. 152). For library activities to take place, the

director establishes personal contact with his staff and creates

the psychological climate to communicate effectively. Once in-

tegrated and harmonious working conditions exist, the director can

send messages to his staff, and they can be invited to express

opinions and feelings. He shows concern for the welfare of his

14

staff, who can be expected to show concern in return.   Staff
loyalty underlies staff morale within the library.

   Cooperation results from staff satisfaction.   A staff member
wants to feel secure and to be liked as a person.   The development
of cooperation and good will is also the responsibility of the
leader.   Actual tools of communication are no substitute for good
leadership.

   The leader is generous with honest praise for work well done.
He is also constructive in pointing out weakness if performance
must be improved.   Using proper techniques of communication, the
library supervisor gives subordinates opportunity to express their
analysis of the reasons for unsatisfactory performance.   Thus,
communication provokes understanding of individual duty and responsibility.   Mutual understanding will help toward the improvement of service.   Good communication is important in achiev-
ing the major library objective which is to provide high-grade
library service.   It is of fundamental importance in any effort to
administer successfully at any level in the organization of an
academic library.   In conclusion, as Emery states, "communication
is central to organization activity and is the basic process upon
which functions depend for their working and contributions to
library goals" (1975, p. 16).

**The last few para-
graphs form the
conclusion. They
refer to the main
point of the whole
paper.**

**The concluding quo-
tation refers directly
to the claim ex-
pressed in the thesis
statement.**

**Quotation, with cita-
tion**

15

Center the heading.

Bibliography

**"Bibliography" is
used as the heading
here, since some
items listed are not
directly mentioned in
the paper.**

**Double space be-
tween all lines.**

**Indent three spaces
for all lines except
the first line of each
entry.**

Abel, M.D. (1968). Aspects of upward communication in a public

   library. In P. Wasserman & M.L. Bundy (Eds.), Reader in

   Library Administration. Washington: Microcard Editions.

Beach, D.S. (1975). Personnel: The management of people at work

   (3rd ed.). New York: Macmillan.

Boaz, M. (Ed.). (1979). Current concepts in library management.

   Colorado: Libraries Unlimited.

Carlson, A. (1979). Communication is tougher than you think.

   Catholic Library World, 50, 331-333.

Emery, R. (1975). Staff communication in libraries. London:

   Bingley.

Forgotson, J. (1960). Communication in the library. Wilson

   Library Bulletin, 34, 425-428.

Goldhaber, G.M. (1976). Communication variables in organizations.

   In B. Cassata & R. Palmer (Eds.), Reader in Library

   Communication. Englewood: Information Handling Services.

Lyle, G.R. (1974). The administration of the college library (4th

   ed.). New York: Wilson.

Rogers, R., & Weber, D. (1971). University library administration.

   New York: Wilson.

Stebbins, K.B., & Mohrhardt, F. E. (1966). Personnel administra-

   tion in libraries (2nd ed.). New York: Scarecrow.

Stueart, R.D., & Eastlick, J. T. (1977). Library management.

   Colorado: Libraries Unlimited.

◧▨▷ UNIT 17
Research Papers in MLA and Scientific Formats

Two sample research papers are given in the following pages to illustrate alternative formats for writing research papers.

The paper by Mario Vespa follows a format adapted from the Modern Language Association (MLA) recommendations. This style is often used in humanities subjects. Its main difference from the APA style is in the use of a separate notes page. Punctuation of the bibliography is also different from the APA style.

The paper by Tzernghong Lin is in a common scientific format in which sections are numbered and reference entries are numbered. Citations are in-text, using the numbers of the reference entries.

Whichever style you follow, remember that the important thing is consistency. Do not mix styles. For instance, do not, in the same paper, number the bibliography entries (scientific style) and also use APA punctuation or MLA footnote pages. Stick to one format only.

Cover page

Title

How Computers Were Born

Author

by

Mario Osvaldo Vespa

Class, instructor, place, date

ELI 4X

Instructor: Peggy Andersen

University of Pittsburgh

April 5, 1982

This page is not numbered.

<u>Outline</u>

<u>Thesis statement</u>: Although the apparent beginning of computers
was about forty years ago, the real history of them starts as long
ago as human life appeared on earth.

    I. Elementary calculators
        A. Hands (fingers)
        B. Stones

   II. Mechanical calculators
        A. Abacus
        B. John Napier's device
        C. William Oughtred's invention: slide rule
        D. Blaise Pascal's machine
        E. Leibnitz's machine
        F. Jacquard punched cards
        G. Charles Babbage
            1. difference engine
            2. analytical engine
        H. Barbour's machine
        I. Baldwin's machine
        J. Hollerith's machine

 III. Semi-electronic calculators
        Mark series

  IV. Electronic calculators
        A. ENIAC
        B. EDVAC
        C. BINAC
        D. UNIVAC
        E. Other computers

**Numbers and letters
show comparative
importance of differ-
ent sections.**

**This page is not
numbered.**

Title repeated on page one.

How Computers Were Born

Brief quotation used to start the paper.

"The electronic digital computer is the latest tool in man's long search for better and faster ways to put numbers to work for

Raised number 1 indicates first footnote.

him."[1] This quotation expresses the common idea that computers are a recent invention, but the idea is really too simplified.

Thesis statement (controlling idea).

Although the apparent beginning of computers was about forty years ago, the real history of them starts as long ago as human life appeared on earth.

Let us go back through time until a few thousand years B.C. when people used to show their fingers while they were referring to the number of persons in their families or to animals that they had hunted. Thus, there was a natural pause when they arrived at five, and a longer one when they arrived at ten, because they had only ten fingers. This fact was the beginning of considering ten as a counting basis. If our hands had had eight fingers, certainly the basis of counting would have been eight instead of

Raised number 2 indicates second footnote.

ten.[2] Thinking about mathematical concepts, the number twelve would been better than ten since it is divisible by two, three, four and six, but, using our hands to count, twelve is a very hard unit to handle. However, the activities of man became more and more complex very quickly, and his ten units grew to twenty when he used his fingers and toes. Nevertheless, these units were not enough to handle his world.

So, a giant step in counting appeared, when prehistoric

1

Page number starts on this page. Only page 1 has the number at the bottom of the page.

**Numbers are at top
right of each page.**

man started to group rough stones at first, and pebbles later, to

represent members of his tribe or enemies whose number was more

than twenty. In some agricultural tribes, they put pebbles in

front of the granary that represented the total amount of grain

stored in it. At the same time that the grains were stored, they

added pebbles to the set. On the other hand, when grains were

consumed, they took pebbles away. This was the very beginning of

the abacus, the first real digital counting machine.

Despite its Latin origin, the word "abacus" is derived from

the Greek word "abax" (about five hundred years B.C.). This type

of calculator was used by the Chinese as early as 2600 B.C. The

Greeks and Romans used pebbles or discs of bone, glass, or ivory,

whose names were "pessoi" or "calculi," and they set them on flat

tables. This is precisely the meaning of "abax": "a flat sur-

face."[3] In addition, a flat panel used to decorate a wall was

called an "abacus." The earlier abacuses were constituted from

**Raised number 3 in-
dicates third foot-
note.**

small pebbles that could move freely in grooves carved in a piece

of wood or in a metal surface. Later,the pebbles or discs were

set into the grooves by means of a piece of wire through them.

In the thirteenth century new elements replaced the pebbles.

They were named "jetons" and they were discs of metal used to

compute amounts. Depending on the country where they were used,

they had different inscriptions on their surfaces.

3

This paper is or-
ganized chronologi-
cally, so there are
many transitions re-
ferring to time se-
quences (such as
"next," "later," and
"then").

The next important event was that, in 1617, John Napier, who
became very famous, developed the logarithmic tables and, at the
same time, a mechanical device commonly known as "Napier's bones."
This name was due to the fact that his machine consisted of some
strips of bones with numbers painted on their surfaces. The
Napier's bones machine was able to do simple multiplications.

Four years later, in 1621, and based on logarithmic principles, William Oughtred invented the Slide Rule. This small
calculator was used just to multiply and divide. Still, the
results obtained with it were not exact, but they were approximate
to the real ones.

Then came a more efficient invention, a gear-driven machine.
The father of the first gear-driven adding machine was Blaise
Pascal, who created it in 1642. Basically it was a wooden box
with a series of open windows under which there were drums, each
one numbered from zero to nine, on its cylindrical surface. These
drums were turned by an equal number of wheels outside the box.
The way the wheels and drums were joined was by means of gears,
whose geared relation was such that when a wheel twisted a complete turn, that is, ten units, the wheel placed at its left side
turned only one unit. The right wheel represented the unit, and,
going toward the left, the other wheels were successively the
tenth, hundredth, thousandth, and so forth.[4]

The middle pages of this sample paper have been omitted.

Later, the integrated circuits replaced the transistor and a new family of computers was born: the third generation. The IBM 360 and CDC 6600 machines belong to this group. Finally, with the appearance of LSI (large-scale integrators) the third generation moved aside for the fourth one.

To conclude, this brief history tells us how the computer has been growing from its birth to the present. It evolved very slowly at first, but the speed of development increased in an exponential way. Thus, behind the evident, very recent revolution in calculating machines from 1944 until now, there is another, not too visible but real one, that constitutes the true origin of modern calculators and that is the human being himself.

Final sentence refers back to the controlling idea.

10

Notes

Use raised numbers for each note.

Double space between notes.

Write only author's last name and page number for later references to the same work.

Do not write author's last name first.

Place publication information in parentheses.

[1]I.J. Seligsohn. <u>Your Career in Computer Programming</u> (New York: Julian Messner, 1967), p. 25.

[2]Seligsohn, p. 26.

[3]J.M. Pullan. <u>The History of the Abacus</u> (New York: Frederick A. Praeger, 1969), p. 17.

[4]J.A.V. Turck. <u>Origin of Modern Calculating Machines</u> (Chicago: Western Society of Engineers, 1921), p. 11.

11

BIBLIOGRAPHY

Capvett, P. "Business Data Processing." Byte and Bit
    Occasional Papers, No. 2 (1983), pp. 10-22.

Carver, D.K. Introduction to Business Data Processing.
    Sacramento, California: Sacramento City College, 1979.

Goldstine, Herman H. The Computer: from Pascal to von
    Neumann. New Jersey: Princeton University Press.
    Princeton, 1973.

Gruenberger, F., Ed. Fourth Generation Computers: User Re-
    quirements and Transition. Englewood Cliffs, New Jersey:
    Informatics Inc., 1970.

Gupton, Ronald P. "The Newest in Information Processing."
    Electronic Review, 23, No. 5 (1983), 29-39.

Howlett, J. and Giancarlo Rota. A History of Computing in
    the Twentieth Century. Los Alamos, New Mexico:
    Metropolis, 1980.

Lubkin, Samuel. Theory of Mathematical Machines. New York:
    New York University Press, 1956.

Maisel, Herbert. Introduction to Electronic Digital Computers.
    New York: McGraw-Hill Book Company, 1969.

Nussbaum, Martin. Opportunities in Electronic Data Processing.
    New York: Universal Publishing and Distribution
    Corporation, 1972.

Pullan, J.M. The History of the Abacus. New York: Frederick
    A. Praeger, 1969.

Seligsohn, I.J. Your Chance in Computer Programming. New
    York: Julian Messner, 1967.

Stern, Nancy. From ENIAC to UNIVAC: An Appraisal of the
    Eckert-Mauchly Computers. Bedford, MA: Digital Press,
    1981.

Thomas, Shirley. Computers: Their History, Present Appli-
    cations, and Future. New York: Holt, Rinehart and
    Winston, 1965.

Turck, J.A.V. Origin of Modern Calculating Machines. Chicago:
    Western Society of Engineers, 1921.

Last name of author is written first. (Only for first author)

Single space within entries. Double space between entries.

Capitalize major words in titles.

Underline book titles.

Do not underline article titles. Place them in quotation marks.

Underline the names of journals.

Use p. and pp. in article citation only when no volume number is given.

Cover page

Title

Software Fault Tolerance

Author

Tzernghong Lin

**Class, instructor,
place, and date**

Linguistics 9
Instructor: Lionel Menasche

Spring Term, 1982
University of Pittsburgh

Page counting starts
on this page. Start
writing page num-
bers from next page.

Thesis statement

     The proposed approach using an operation chain to detect
control faults can provide automation to check execution sequence,
so that the inefficient and unreliable implementation of checking
capability by the human programmer can be avoided.

Outline

Outline uses a num-
bering system also
used in the paper it-
self.

1.   Introduction

    1.1. Software development

    1.2. Fault tolerance in software

The middle part of this outline has been omitted.

4.   Error Recovery

    4.1. State restoration

    4.2. Removal of the failed unit

    4.3. System backup

5.   A Proposed Approach

    5.1. Model of operation

    5.2. Theory: Forward/backward verification

    5.3. Operation chain

    5.4. Event handling

    5.5. Configuration of processors

6.   Conclusion

References

3

**Sections are num-
bered and have
headings.**

1.   Introduction

In the real-time systems like nuclear power plants, mis-
sile defense systems and air controller systems, the failure
of a system may be disastrous. The causes of system failure
come from software faults, hardware failure and operational
errors by humans. The reliability of hardware has been improved by more reliable parts and component redundancy, so
the system can tolerate occasional failures of internal com-

**Citations are in
brackets and use
numbers that refer
to the reference list
at the end of the pa-
per.**

ponents and modules [1].

However, hardware failure is only one source of unreli-
ability in computing systems. The importance of software
reliability has been realized since the computer system became more complex and in this paper I suggest an approach to

Thesis statement.

improving reliability. The proposed approach using an operation chain to detect control faults can provide automation
to check execution sequence, so the inefficient and unreliable implementation of checking capability by the human
programmer can be avoided.

Section heading.

1.1. Software development

In constructing system software, there are two ways to
enhance software reliability. One is to reduce software
errors before the system is put into operation. The other
is to offer protective software redundancy to tolerate

Second citation.

faults during operation [2].

The development of software usually undergoes the

4

following phases:

1) Application Requirement Specifications

2) Software Requirement Specifications

3) Design and Analysis

4) Software Implementation

5) Model Testing

6) Software Defenses Instrumentation

7) System Integration and Validation

8) Documentation [3] .   **Third citation.**

Errors are often induced in specification, design and implementation, while they are found and corrected by testing
and validating [4] .   **Fourth citation.**

The construction of a large system is very complicated,
and the software cannot be expected to be error-free, no
matter how carefully the system is designed and implemented.
Although the software errors can be exposed by program de-
bugging and testing, there is no way to prove that a large
program does not have any error [5] . As a result, there is   **Fifth citation.**
always a limitation on reliability which can be achieved by
program verification.

1.2. Fault tolerance in software

More reliable systems can be achieved by software fault
tolerance. In software fault tolerance, protective redundancy is added to functional components, i.e. codes and
data, to cope with software errors and other system faults.

5

The middle pages of this sample paper have been omitted.

5.5. Configuration of processors

Using several processors, the system can have the self-check capability to cover all of the control faults that may appear in the system. As shown in fig. 5.4., these processors check one another to verify the operations.

Figures and tables are numbered in accordance with the section number.

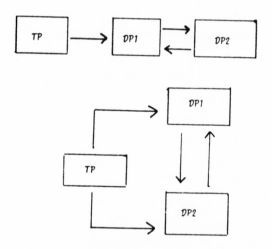

Fig. 5.5. Two possible configurations of processors

15

The above configurations ensure every operation of the active components in the system is verified.

6. Conclusion

Software fault tolerance has been developed over the past ten years. However, most of the techniques invented so far are ad hoc and are tailored to specific systems [5] . There are no general rules for building a system with the capability of software fault tolerance. The proposed approach which uses an operation chain to detect control fault and software integrity can be used to implement a system with intensive checking capability. The automation of insertion or removal of checking capabilities [5] can be attained by designing a new compiler for the system. This compiler can trace the operation chain of the program, and produce the corresponding linking information according to the control sequence. The verification of control sequence can be performed by either software or hardware controller. Considering the efficiency of execution, a hardware controller is preferred for the system. Due to the inherent need for software fault tolerance, smarter features can be expected in the future techniques of constructing a robust system.

Citation (number 5 in reference list).

Final paragraph refers back to the general idea of the thesis statement.

Citation (number 5 in reference list).

References   16

Entries are numbered and listed in order of mention in the paper. (Reference list is not alphabetized but could be.)

Single space within entries. Double space between entries.

Underline book titles and journal names.

Last names of all authors are written first.

Titles have only the first letter of the first word capitalized.

[1]   Randell, B. System structure for software fault tolerance. <u>Proceeding International Conference on Reliable Software</u>, April 1975, 450-457.

[2]   Avizienis, Algirdes. Fault-tolerance and fault-intolerance: Complementary approaches to reliable computing. <u>Proceeding International Conference on Reliable Software</u>, April 1975, 458-464.

[3]   Ramamoorthy, C.V. & Ho, S.F. Testing large software with automated software evaluation systems. <u>IEEE Transactions on Software Engineering</u>, March 1975, <u>SE-1</u>, 46-58.

[4]   Yan, Stephen S. & Chen, Fu-Chung. An approach to concurrent control flow checking. <u>IEEE Transactions on Software Engineering</u>, March 1980, <u>SE-6</u>, 126-137.

[5]   Yan S.S. & Cheung, R.C. Design of self-checking software. <u>Proceeding International Conference on Reliable Software</u>, April 1975, 450-457.

[6]   Taylor, David J., Morgan, David E. & Black, James P. Redundancy in data structures: Improving software fault tolerance. <u>IEEE Transactions on Software Engineering</u>, November 1980, <u>SE-6</u>, 585-594.

[7]   Randell, B. System structure for software fault tolerance. <u>IEEE Transactions on Software Engineering</u>, March 1975, <u>SE-1</u>, 220-232.

[8]   Cristian, Flaviu. Exception handling and software fault tolerance. <u>IEEE Transactions on Computers</u>, June 1982, <u>C-31</u>, 531-540.

[9]   Ramamoorthy, C.V. & Cheung, R.C. Integrity of Large Software Systems. <u>3rd Annual Texas Conference on Computing Systems</u>, 1974.

[10] Knuth, D.E. <u>The art of computer programming</u>, Vol. 1 - <u>Fundamental algorithms, 2nd ed.</u> Reading, MA: Addison-Wesley, 1973.

[11] Wei, A., Hiraishi, K., Cheng R. & Campbell, R. Application of the fault-tolerant deadline mechanism to a satellite on-board computer system. <u>UIUCDCS-R-80-1025</u>, Dept. of CS, Univ. of Ill. at Urbana-Champaign.

Some Frequent Student Questions

Certain questions come up very frequently in a class in which students are learning to write research papers and reports. These questions are listed below and are followed by the answers that they usually get. These answers give an insight into the usual requirements of academic courses. When they refer to the specific requirements of assignments in this textbook, this is made clear.

1. HOW LONG SHOULD MY PAPER BE?

To this question, many instructors give the vague answer: "As long as it needs to be in order to say what you have to say." This leaves inexperienced student writers puzzled, because they usually think that a paper is not a research paper if it is very short. In fact, academic research papers and reports vary greatly in length, from "short" (1–6 pages of double spaced typescript) to "medium" (7–15 pages) to "long (15–40 pages). If your instructor does not give you upper and lower page limits, then you should think in terms of a medium length paper. A very short student paper is unlikely to be thorough and complete, and a very long one will not be impressive just because it is long. The most effective paper is both complete and concise.

2. HOW MANY NOTECARDS SHOULD I WRITE?

There is no specific number that is best. In academic courses, the instructor never sees your cards, so you can write them as you wish and you can write as many as you wish. You do not even have to use cards if you prefer sheets of paper, but the card system has been found by many writers to be a very efficient one, especially for the drafting and redrafting stage when they are frequently changing the order of ideas. As a rough guideline, it may help you to think that a typical medium length paper will be based on 70 to 100 note cards, but this varies according to the subject, the writer, and the books and articles the writer has immediately at hand when actually writing. You should always think of note taking as having two equally important purposes: the obvious one of recording information, and the one which is sometimes forgotten—writing notes is a way of understanding the information and organizing it in one's mind.

3. MUST MY PAPER BE TYPED?

It is not essential to have your paper typed unless the instructor makes a special point of requesting it. The important thing when handwriting a paper is that your writing must be easy to read. You must not put the reader in a position of having to struggle to read your handwriting. The easier it is to read, the happier your instructor will be. And instructors are only human! They are influenced by such things, even if only subconsciously. Indeed some researchers have shown that a typed composition will, on average, be scored 10% higher than a handwritten one, but without this being a conscious intention of the scorers—a point worth thinking about, even though, as said earlier, typing is not essential. Graduate students are more often expected to type their papers than undergraduates. In every case find out exactly what each instructor wants.

4. I'VE SEEN SOME STUDENTS HAND IN THEIR PAPERS IN FANCY PLASTIC COVERS WITH BINDINGS. SHOULD I DO THIS TOO?

No. The fancy cover makes no difference to the quality of the writing and research. A cover sheet (as in the examples in earlier units of this book) is quite enough. However, if you think about the answer given above in regard to typing versus handwriting, you may begin to believe that there could be a subconscious influence on the reader. Think about it and decide for yourself.

5. HOW MANY BOOKS AND ARTICLES MUST I USE FOR MY PAPER?

There is no ''must'' on this issue. Some research papers use many, others very few. Some papers refer only to articles. Others refer only to books, but, if the papers are very up-to-date, they usually include references to a few recent articles as well as to books. For some types of research paper that report experimental results in scientific fields, there may be no references at all, but this is very rare because such results are usually described in the context of previously published research. For the type of student paper discussed in this textbook, there should probably be a minimum of about four or five references to books or articles.

6. DOES THIS TEXTBOOK CONTAIN ALL I NEED IN ORDER TO WRITE PAPERS FOR MY ACADEMIC COURSES IN THE CORRECT FORMAT?

No, it does not. There is probably enough here for most undergraduate papers, but graduate students should obtain a copy of the style guide required for their specialized areas, especially when they are getting close to writing their theses or dissertations. Find out from your professors what the preferred style guides are.

7. HOW DO I KNOW WHICH STYLE TO USE—MLA OR APA OR SCIENTIFIC OR SOME OTHER?

Ask your academic advisor or course professors or advanced graduate students in your subject area what the standard requirements are.

8. WHEN TYPING OR HANDWRITING HOW MANY SPACES SHOULD I LEAVE BETWEEN LINES?

When typing it is customary to double space and when handwriting you should leave one line blank between each line of writing. This makes it easier for the instructor to read and also leaves space for the instructor to write comments.

9. SHOULD I WRITE ON BOTH SIDES OF EACH SHEET OF PAPER?

No. Write on one side only. This is usually easier for the reader and it also has an advantage for you. As you write, you are bound to make mistakes or change your mind about some things as you go along; if you write on one side only, you will not have to rewrite so much on these occasions as you would if you were covering both sides. For typewritten papers, you should always use one side only.

10. SHOULD THE THESIS STATEMENT BE PART OF THE PAPER OR JUST WRITTEN SEPARATELY ON A SEPARATE PAGE AT THE BEGINNING?

It must be part of the text of the paper. It is a sentence that appears in one of the introductory paragraphs. When you write it on a separate page at the beginning (as in the sequence of assignments in this textbook), that is only a convenience for the instructor. In your academic courses there is no need to do this unless your instructor specifically asks for it. When an abstract (or summary) is written at the beginning, again only when the instructor wants it, the thesis statement normally appears there also.

11. MUST EVERY PAPER HAVE AN OUTLINE AT THE BEGINNING ON A SEPARATE SHEET, LIKE THE "CONTENTS" PAGE OF A BOOK, TO HELP THE READER?

An outline with numbering and indentation is not normally part of a research paper that you hand in to an instructor in an academic course. In this textbook it was required so that your writing instructor could see how you had organized your paper. In your academic courses, present a separate outline or abstract only if it is requested. The way you have organized the parts and arguments of your paper should always be stated in the introductory paragraphs, where you should write several sentences to explain this. So, in a way, your outline is part of the introduction, but it appears as consecutive sentences in a paragraph and not as the indented and numbered outline that you can use to help organize your thoughts before you write. Letting your reader know the structure of your paper in this way is an essential aid to him or her in setting up a mental framework within which to understand what you have written. In short, you write separate outlines for yourself to structure and develop your own thoughts and you place an "outline" in the mind of your reader as part of the introduction.

12. I DON'T LIKE TO WRITE DETAILED OUTLINES WITH INDENTATION AND NUMBERING, SO WHY SHOULD I DO IT?

You do not have to write formal outlines when producing a paper for your academic courses. In that situation, no one except you would see such outlines anyway. The outline is intended only as a guide to you in your own thinking and writing. A few, very rare, writers are able to keep a clear organization in their minds and not write outlines as they go along, but most of us are not like that. Also, writing down your ideas has a different effect from just thinking about how to organize them. Writing them down triggers other ideas; rereading what you've written also sets new possibilities going in the mind; and a simple renumbering is a quick way to try out new arrangements of ideas. Instead of thinking of outlining as a burden, think of it as the beginning of drafting your paper. Sometimes, an instructor will want to see a formal outline, but in such a case it will be requested. If the formal outline is to be handed in with the final draft, then you can leave its final version till last: write it only after you have completed the final draft. All other outlines are really just temporary things that assist you in the process of writing. They are not ends in themselves. In the sequence of assignments in this book, your preliminary outline and a revised version of it are asked for only so that your instructor can see how you are proceeding with your on-going ideas about the paper. Also it gets you going with thinking and writing, instead of allowing too much time to pass (as it so easily can) in note-taking alone and in vague and unfocused thinking.

13. WHEN SHOULD I USE QUOTATIONS? MUST I ALWAYS USE SOME OR CAN I WRITE A RESEARCH PAPER WITHOUT USING ANY AT ALL?

You should only quote something directly when the way it is expressed is especially effective or unusual. Quotations are not some kind of decoration or required part of a student paper. Indeed you may have no need for any quotations. Many research papers that report experimental results do not have quotations, but papers in the humanities and social sciences usually do because they deal very often the ideas of other writers. To decide whether to paraphrase or quote directly just ask yourself if you are more interested in what is said than how it is said. If it is the content (what is said) that you are interested in, then paraphrase. If it is the manner of expression that is striking, then quote directly. Never quote too much (more than about ten percent of a paper), or your instructor might begin to think that you are using quotations just to fill page!

14. MUST EVERY PAPER PROVE SOMETHING?

No. Only an argumentative paper tries to prove a point. Other papers, reports, do not try to gather evidence and use logical argument to support an assertion that some people might disagree with. When you begin a research paper project, you should have an absolutely clear idea of which type is required of you. Often, undergraduates are asked to write reports, but it is rare for graduate students to do so. The normal requirement for graduates is to write argumentative papers. If you are in doubt about what you have to do, discuss it with your instructor early in the term.

15. WHAT IS THE DIFFERENCE BETWEEN THE "THESIS" OF AN ARGUMENT AND THE USE OF THE TERM "THESIS" IN "THESIS STATEMENT" AND IN "GRADUATE THESIS"?

You have to be careful in using the term "thesis." It has two basic meanings: one is "a proposition presented as an idea to be discussed or proved"; the other (obviously derived from the first) is "a written dissertation required by a college as part of the work towards a higher degree." So the thesis of an argument is the assertion that the argument is trying to prove, the claim that is being supported through evidence and logical statements. This is the meaning that is used in the phrase "thesis statement," which in this textbook refers to the one sentence that expresses the main idea (or proposition) of a research paper. It is also possible to use the phrase more loosely to mean several sentences that express both a summarized argument and the point that the argument is trying to make. This looser usage sometimes appears in dissertations in a section headed "Statement of the Thesis," but, strictly defined, the "thesis statement" is only the assertion that is to be proved and not the argumentation that leads to proof. In the context of a single research paper, the "thesis statement" is synonymous with "thesis sentence," a single, grammatically complete sentence, the main clause of which expresses the idea to be proved or expanded upon. When talking of a "graduate thesis," reference is being made to the written dissertation defined above.

16. WHAT CAN I DO IF I FIND IT IMPOSSIBLE TO REMEMBER ALL THOSE RULES ABOUT CITATION FORMATS, EVEN FOR ONLY ONE STYLE OF PRESENTATION?

Do not even try to remember them. All writers of such papers keep style guides for reference and these are normally used at the *end* of the whole process. That is, you can put your citations in the correct format after you have written the text of the paper, although in the final draft in-text references must be put in as you go along. The format and the "look" of the paper should not be in your mind when you are busy developing ideas, drafting and redrafting. Thinking about the mechanical conventions at this point would only interfere with the flow of activity. However, when you are developing a preliminary bibliography, be sure to note all the information that you will need for a complete citation, so that you will not waste time later going back to the library just to get such information when you can least afford the time.

17. SHOULD I LEAVE OUT INFORMATION THAT I THINK THE INSTRUCTOR KNOWS?

Even though the actual writing situation is that of student and instructor, you should not try to guess at what an individual instructor may or may not know. Rather, imagine that you are writing for readers who are knowledgeable about your general subject but not about the details of your narrowed topic. With this guideline in mind, you will avoid writing too much that is obvious or leaving out some information that is needed. Your reading of the literature in the general subject area will tell you what is generally known and your reading within the narrowed topic area will tell you what very few people are thinking about and writing about. But, when you become familiar with a very limited topic, you can easily take for granted some things that people need to know, so you should give too much rather than too little background information if you are finding it hard to establish the right balance. What this means is that you should think of the instructor as representing a group of readers, a fairly small community of specialists. Even in your English language class, in which the instructor obviously cannot be a specialist in all the disciplines of the various students, you should still write as if for a community of experts in your field. Your English instructor will read your paper for *how* you write it rather than for what you write; the latter is for an academic subject specialist to judge.

18. HOW CAN I BE EXPECTED TO WRITE PAPERS LIKE THOSE IN THE JOURNALS WHEN I AM STILL JUST A STUDENT?

Your instructors do not expect you to do that, but they do hope that your approach to the whole process of research, thinking, and expressing your ideas will be the same as that of the professional academic writers. Also, more is naturally expected of graduates than undergraduates. A research paper written for a graduate academic course should really be quite close to the type and quality of short, published articles.

19. IF I KNOW A LOT ABOUT A SUBJECT FROM MY OWN EXPERIENCE, CAN I WRITE THE RESEARCH PAPER FROM THIS, WITHOUT USING BOOKS AND ARTICLES?

No. If you did that, it would not be a research paper in the usual scholarly sense. Certainly you could use your experience of a special field as a source of ideas for a research paper, for instance, for an idea that you want to prove is true or useful or original. And that idea would be expressed in your thesis statement. Or you might use personal experience as part of the evidence in an argument, but only as a small part because it would be very subjective and, probably, impossible to test scientifically or argue about in a strictly logical way. If you write only from personal experience, you would be writing a personal essay, a composition that would be quite acceptable in another situation (such as a weekly composition for a writing teacher) but not as a research paper. Using books and articles is an integral part of writing a research paper, especially in the humanities and social sciences. In some scientific fields, papers that report the results of experimental research may make no reference to other works, but even in these there is often some attempt to set the information in the context of the work of others.

20. CAN I USE SUBHEADINGS IN A RESEARCH PAPER AND, IF SO, HOW MANY?

In a short paper it is best to avoid all subheadings, unless you are certain that they would help your reader. Using too many can make the paper seem to lack cohesion, because they are not a substitute for effective transitional sentences or paragraphs. The headings ''Introduction'' and ''Conclusion'' are often used when they are not necessary; in a short paper it does not need to be stated that the first few paragraphs are introductory and the last few concluding. In very long papers subheadings can be more useful, but there is no way to calculate a number that is appropriate; each must be judged separately. In some technical and scientific fields, it is normal to use specific subheadings for every paper. You will soon notice which ones you as you read articles in your field and you can find out what is needed from the style guide that is used for that field.

21. WHY ARE RESEARCH PAPERS ASSIGNED IN SO MANY DIFFERENT AC-ADEMIC COURSES?

Reseach papers are the basis of communication between scholars. You can even think of many academic books as consisting of sets of research papers (or articles or chapters) that develop a subject in depth. And in a general way the process of writing a research paper—investigation, analysis, developing and changing ideas, clear self-expression in writing, and learning through writing—is what your colleges and universities are trying to teach you. The following quotations from a recent article effectively summarize the purposes of research papers (Schwegler, R. A. and Shamoon, L. K. (1982). The aims and process of the research paper. *College English, 44,* 817–824):

> What, then, are the aims, structures, and stylistic features of the research papers (or articles) college instructors write and also expect their students to write?
> The aim of the academic research paper is twofold, reflecting the duality of the research process it aims to represent. The research paper is at once open-ended and limited—exploratory and demonstrative. It begins with the known, as defined by current scholarship, and moves into the unknown, attempting to pursue an admittedly elusive ''truth.'' At the same time the statements it makes about the nature of its subjects are generally limited to those whose validity can be demonstrated with a high degree of probability according to the method guiding the inquiry and according to evidence drawn from the subject. This

emphasis on method of investigation is one of the distinguishing features of research writing.

(p. 821)

And though it is open-ended, academic research is not formless, as most of us are aware; it begins with a review of current knowledge and then moves through a variation of one or four basic patterns, which in turn influence the organization of the research paper. These patterns can be distinguished by their relationship to previous scholarly discussion and by the roles filled by the other elements of the research process. The patterns are as follows:

1. *Review of research.* This pattern takes as its subject not some external phenomenon, but the process of scholarly debate itself. It reviews the methods, data, and conclusions of prior research, pointing out emerging patterns of agreement and conflict and attempting through critical analysis to shed new light on the development of research in a particular area.

2. *Application or implementation of a theory.* This pattern consists of the application of a generally accepted theory to a new situation or subject; the theory is generally not questioned, and the burden of proof lies in showing that it can be used to explain or understand the new phenomenon. For example, a theory developed to account for the structure of a specific social group or even a set of poems can often be applied to similar subjects.

3. *Refute, refine, or replicate prior research.* Much research begins when a scholar takes issue with the assertions, data, or methodology of someone else's research. The disagreement leads to a reexamination, a remeasurement, or a reinterpretation, and eventually to a new set of assertions. Other research, related in pattern though not direction, may accept the original research and attempt to corroborate it.

4. *Testing a hypothesis.* This is the classic and in some ways most challenging pattern of research. It begins with the isolation and close observation of a phenomenon, followed by the formulation of tentative assertions about the phenomenon (hypotheses), and concludes with the testing of the assertions through observation and measurement of the phenomenon they purport to describe.

(pp. 822–823)

 APPENDIX I

Form used by instructors in the English Language Institute, University of Pittsburgh, to record student progress through the assignments in this textbook. Variations are made on the form to suit different student and instructor needs:

English Language Institute
Research Paper Progress Report

Student's Name _____

Class and Section _____   Term _____

Research Paper Topic: General _____

Narrowed _____

STEP	DATE HANDED IN	COMMENTS (complete, on time, correct form, etc.)	POINTS
1. Reference Sources			
2. Preliminary bibliography			
3. Preliminary thesis and outline			
4. Note Cards			
5. Revised thesis and outline			
6. Sample Draft (two pages)			
7. Preliminary Draft			
8. Final Draft			

Further Comments:

Total Points: _____

Grade: _____

Please return this form to the student advisor at the end of the term.

 # APPENDIX II

Typical schedule of due dates for assignments. This refers to one fifteen-week term in which the research paper is one-third of the work load of the writing class. Instructors vary these dates as appropriate to different groups of students. This schedule is given to students at the beginning of term.

Linguistics 4/9

TERM PAPER SCHEDULE

Winter Term

	Due Date	*Points*
Topic (General Subject Area) (Unit 2)	Thurs. 1/20	—
Topic (Narrowed to Specific Aspect) (Unit 4)	Thurs. 1/27	—
Reference Sources (Unit 5)	Tues. 2/1	—
Preliminary Bibliography (Unit 6)	Thurs. 2/3	10
Preliminary Thesis and Outline (Units 7 & 8)	Tues. 2/8	5
Note Cards (Unit 10)	Tues. 2/22	10
Revised Thesis and Outline (Units 11 & 12)	Tues. 3/8	10
Sample Draft (two pages) (Unit 13)	Tues. 3/15	10
Preliminary Draft (Unit 14)	Tues. 3/22	30
Final Draft (Unit 15)	Tues. 3/29	25
		100

Answer Keys for Exercises

UNIT 3, Exercise 3 (b): Alphabetization Exercise

1. al-Arabi, Mohammed
2. Bander, Robert G.
3. Barnard, Helen
4. Crowell, Thomas Lee
5. d'Angelo, Frank
6. Dubin, Fraida
7. El-Osman, Ali
8. Frank, Marcella
9. Hall, Alan T.
10. Hall, Albert Peter
11. Hall, Edward T.
12. Loringhoven, Heinz von
13. Mao, Tse-Tung
14. Matsushita, Yoko
15. McTaggart, Hamish Angus
16. Merwe, Hendrik van der
17. O'Hara, P. R.
18. Olshtain, Elite
19. Ortega, Xavier
20. Orwell, George
21. Peterkin, Peter P.
22. Pollock, Carroll Washington
23. Proyart, Pierre de
24. Rios, Jaime de los
25. Smith, James R.
26. Smith, John
27. Walker, JoEllen
28. Wang, Minn-Hu
29. Williams, F.
30. Zelman, P. George

UNIT 3, Exercise 4: Call Number Exercise

(a) Philosophy-Religion
(b) Line 3 (F2)
(c) No, because a year is included (1978)
(d) At least 14 (c14)

UNIT 3, Exercise 5: Readers' Guide to Periodical Literature Exercise

(a) R. M. Galvin
(b) September, 1982
(c) Drawing with colored pencils
(d) Musicals, Reviews—Single Works
(e) Pages 100 to 107
(f) Yes

UNIT 6, Exercise 1: Bibliographical Citations Exercise

(a) Hatch, E., & Farhady, H. (1982). *Research design and statistics for applied linguistics.* Rowley, MA: Newbury House.
(b) Investigator, I. M. (1934). Types of clay used in ancient Acapulcan pottery. *History of Applied Technology Quarterly, 86,* 119–123.

UNIT 6, Exercise 2: Bibliographical Citations Exercise

(a) Author's initials should follow last name.
(b) Do not underline article title.
(c) No capital letter on title words in this style (except for first letter and first letter after colon).
(d) Colon, not comma, between place and publisher.
(e) Date in wrong place.
(f) Underline title of book.
(g) Place period after title.
(h) Put in a date.
(i) Volume number should be underlined/italicized.
(j) Place of publication should follow title.
(k) No quotation marks for title in APA style.
(l) Indent second line three spaces.

UNIT 7, Exercise 1: Thesis Statements Exercise

1. ATS	6. NT	11. RTS	16. ATS
2. NT	7. ATS	12. ATS	17. ATS
3. ATS	8. NT	13. ATS	18. RTS
4. GT	9. TRS	14. GT	19. ATS
5. GT	10. RTS	15. RTS	20. ATS

UNIT 7, Exercise 2: Thesis Statements Exercise

(a) Argumentative (because it makes a prediction about the future).
(b) Report (because it does not make a claim that anyone would disagree with).
(c) Argumentative (because it makes a surprising claim about two fields not normally associated).
(d) Report (because the claim is a generally accepted one).
(e) Argumentative (because there is still some uncertainty about the claim: the author uses the word "may").
(f) Argumentative *or* Report (depending on how the phrase "management information system" is understood: If it is a nontechnical, general term, then probably nobody would argue with the claim (Report); if the term has a specialized, technical meaning, then the claim probably needs to be proved (Argumentative); a specialist in information science must determine which applies).

UNIT 9: Plagiarism Exercise

1. Not P   Direct quotation is acceptable.
2. P   Needs quotation marks.
3. P   Except for last four quoted words, because retains original grammar.
4. Not P   Acceptable paraphrase.
5. Not P   Idea is attributed to author, paraphrase and direct quotation are acceptable.
6. P   Needs quotation marks.
7. Not P   Acceptable paraphrase.
8. Not P   Acceptable paraphrase and clear attribution of idea to author.

Glossary

The terms in this glossary have been selected to assist with understanding both this text and other terminology commonly met in research paper writing. Many entries have been suggested by students in the English Language Institute, University of Pittsburgh. Some of the definitions are based on those in *The American Heritage Dictionary of the English Language*.

A

abbreviation   a shortened form of a word or phrase

abstract   a summary

academic   related to school and schoolwork

acknowledgment   statement of the source of an idea or quotation; full acknowledgment is made in research papers of the sources of ideas, information and quotations; without this, one could be accused of PLAGIARISM

afterword   a statement at the end of a composition or text, but not part of the main text

alphabetical order   special sequencing of words or names according to the order of letters in the alphabet and based on the series of letters in the spelling of the word or name

alphabetize   to arrange in order of the letters of a language; with words or names, the first letter of each takes priority, followed by the second letter of each, and so on

analysis   separation of a whole into its parts, usually with the aim of gaining more insight into the whole and/or the parts; in writing, a possible way of organizing information; also called DIVISION

annual   a periodical published each year

anonymous   without a known author

APA   abbreviation of ''American Psychological Association''; this Association publishes a style guide that is widely used in the social sciences

appendix   a separate section of subsidiary or supplementary material at the end of a book

Arabic numerals   the symbols 1, 2, 3, 4, 5, 6, 7, 8, 9, 0 used to express numbers [compare: ROMAN NUMERALS]

argument   discussion in which disagreement is expressed; debate; discussion of opposing points

argumentative thesis statement   thesis statement expressing a point of view that in some way opposes other points of view; a thesis statement making a claim or assertion that needs to be supported with evidence

argumentative research paper   a research paper that uses evidence and argumentation to support an assertion made by the author; in this type of paper, the author expresses an opinion that some would disagree with and then tries to show why this view is preferable to others; may be contrasted with a "report," which is also based on informational research but which does not express its author's opinion [compare: CRITIQUE]

article   a short, written composition explaining or arguing something; typically published in journals or newspapers; several articles by the same author or by different authors may be published together as a book

assert   to state something as if it is true

assignment   something given as a task

audience   a group of readers, listeners, or spectators; the assumed audience of a research paper is readers who have a similar background to the writer; the actual audience of a student paper is the instructor, but the paper is normally expressed as if written by one authority for other authorities

audiovisual   related to library or classroom materials presenting information that can be heard as well as seen; often a combination of audiotape and/or videotape and written text

author   the writer of a composition, paper, essay, or book

author card   in a library catalog, a card alphabetized according to the author's last name

author/date documentation   the style of source documentation which includes author, date, and page references in the body of the text, in parentheses, and which does not have separate footnotes; sometimes called IN-TEXT DOCUMENTATION; information in parentheses, together with the bibliography, gives a complete reference; author/date documentation is becoming more and more commonly used in academic publications

author number   part of a library book's call number; also called the BOOK NUMBER

authority   a expert in a particular field of knowledge; the source of expert knowledge; a citation from an expert source

B **bibliography**   a list of written works consulted for a book or article, usually placed at the end of it; a list of works on a specific subject; a list of works by one writer; in research paper writing, a preliminary bibliography is a list of works that are potentially useful and a final bibliography is the list of works that were actually consulted; a research paper bibliography usually includes works not directly mentioned in the text, but which were consulted for background [compare: REFERENCE]

bibliography card   a card with information (author, publisher, etc.) about one work; in research paper writing, each bibliography card refers to a work consulted by the writer of the paper

biennial referring to a publication, one which appears every two years [contrast: "biannual"—appearing twice each year]

biography a history of someone's life

block indentation of a series of lines in a text; a long quotation is usually blocked, with no quotation marks, to set it off from the rest of the text

block letter same as CAPITAL LETTER

body the central or main part of anything; in a paper, usually refers to all the text except for the introductory and concluding paragraphs

book a written or printed volume by one or many authors; does not refer to a journal, periodical, or magazine containing short articles by different authors, but can refer to a selected collection of such articles produced as a one-time publication

book number part of a library book's call number; also called the AUTHOR NUMBER

browse to inspect in a leisurely or casual way; often refers to looking at books, etc., in a library or bookstore

C **call number** number used to locate a book in a library; usually either the LIBRARY OF CONGRESS or the DEWEY DECIMAL SYSTEM is used

capital letter a letter of the alphabet written in a larger (and sometimes different) form, as compared to its SMALL LETTER version; an upper-case letter

card a small, flat piece of stiff paper; file cards are often used in research paper writing for bibiography entries and note-taking to simplify reordering of references and written information

card catalog in a library, a series of files with cards listing book publication information (author, title), subject and location in the library

catalog [also spelled "catalogue"] a list of items, sometimes with a brief description of each item

cause and effect in writing, a possible way of organizing the information in a paragraph or composition ["cause" = something responsible for a result; "effect" = a result produced by something]

centered heading a heading placed in the center of a line, with equal blank space on each side of it; used for short papers [compare: SIDE HEADING and PARAGRAPH HEADING]

chart in a book or paper, a page on which information is presented in the form of diagrams, graphs, or tables

cite (v) [citation (n)] to mention as an authority or example, usually in order to support an argument; in a research paper, citations are references to authors quoted or mentioned and are part of the DOCUMENTATION

claim a statement of something as a fact

class number   part of a library book's call number, indicating which subject area the book falls into

classification   arrangement according to groups with shared features; in writing a possible way of organizing information

clause   a group of words containing a subject and a predicate that forms part of a compound or complex sentence

closed stacks   library area that is not open to borrowers; library shelves from which books may be obtained through a librarian, usually by filling out a request form; rare or valuable collections are usually kept in closed stacks [contrast: OPEN STACKS]

coherence   in writing, the quality of parts being logically connected with each other, even when transitional (cohesive) elements are not used; in general, making sense or having meaning

cohesion   in writing, the quality of having parts (such as sentences or paragraphs) connected with each other by means of transitional (cohesive) elements, such as transitional words, phrases, sentences, or paragraphs; even if such connecting elements are present, in text, in part or whole, may lack coherence

comparison   description of similarities and differences in two or more things; in writing, a way of arranging information [compare: CONTRAST]

compile (v) [compilation (n)]   to gather into one list or book; to collect items from several sources for a list or for a body of information; for example, notes or bibliographical references may be compiled

composing process   the activities that take place before and during writing; sometimes described as: pre-writing (or incubation), writing, revising, and editing; the parts of the process do not follow a strict linear order, but are cyclic and sometimes cannot be distinguished from each other; like other complex cognitive processes, especially creative ones, little is known about what happens in the mind during composing; discourse plans are repeatedly made and changed during composing

composition   in reference to writing, a short essay; the arrangement of constituent parts

conclusion   in a composition, the final paragraph(s), usually restating the thesis or summarizing the main points

condense (v) [condensation (n)]   to decrease in length or size; to summarize; to make shorter; to abridge

conference   a meeting for consultation or discussion; a professional conference is a meeting of specialists at which scholarly papers are presented orally

conference proceedings   a publication containing in printed form the papers delivered orally at a conference

connectors   same as TRANSITIONS

consult   to seek information or advice from; refer to for information; researchers consult sources for information or ideas

context   what comes before or after certain words or certain passages; the context contributes to how elements of language are interpreted; the same words may have different meanings in different contexts

contrast a type of comparison in which differences between two or more things are pointed out; in writing, a way of arranging information

controlling idea in a research paper, the main idea expressed in the THESIS STATEMENT; the central notion or concept that indicates the scope of the paper

copyright exclusive legal right to publish, sell, or distribute written or artistic work

copyright date the date when a publication was legally registered in copyright; use the most recent copyright date as the date of publication of a book which has been published in more than one edition

copyright page the page, usually following the title page, that gives copyright information (such as date, publisher, and publishing history)

cover sheet a page attached to the front of a paper or report on which are written the date, the author's name, the title and, if for a school course, the instructor's name and the course number

cover page same as COVER SHEET

critique a review or commentary that carefully evaluates something; the writer expresses personal judgments about the object of the critique and tries to support those judgements with evidence and logical reasoning

cross-reference an indication to a reader about further information elsewhere; for example, an entry in an index may refer the reader to another section of the index to find related entries under a different heading; cross-references also appear in bibliographies and footnotes

D **date of publication** the year in which a publication first appeared, usually given on the copyright page

debate discussion of opposing points; formal argumentation about an issue

definition (n) [define (v)] a statement of the meaning or contents of something; formal definition consists of stating the general class (or species) to which something belongs and then stating how it is different from other things in that class; in writing, a way of organizing information

descriptor a label (word or phrase) that serves as a subject area heading in an information storage system

Dewey decimal classification system a way of arranging books in a library, with numbers referring to subject areas; some college libraries still use this system, but it is becoming less widely found

000	General Works	500	Pure Science
100	Philosophy	600	Useful Arts
200	Religion	700	Fine Arts
300	Social Science	800	Literature
400	Language	900	History

These ten categories are further divided, with a numerical coding, into: country, language used, type of literature, and period in literature. A librarian will help you find the exact coding of interest to you.

diagram a drawing or plan designed to show visually the relationships between parts of a whole

dictionary a reference list of words, with definitions and other information such as pronunciation; a monolingual dictionary is all in one language; a bilingual dictionary gives translation equivalents from one language to another

discipline a branch of knowledge or of teaching

discourse long, formal expression of something in either speech or writing

discovery draft the first draft of a composition, written in such a way as to allow thoughts to flow out freely without inhibition, the aim being to "discover" ideas and connections between ideas; the subconscious, creative part of the mind is allowed free play in this way; such drafts are not written to be read by anyone other than the author, who deliberately ignores spelling and correct grammar; see FREE WRITING and WRITER'S BLOCK

dissertation a long written work on an academic subject; usually refers to such a work written for a university doctoral degree [compare: THESIS]

division breaking a subject into smaller parts; in writing, a possible way of organizing information; also called ANALYSIS

document (v) [documentation (n)] to acknowledge in writing, as in footnotes and bibliography, all the sources used in preparing a paper

document sheet of paper with written evidence, proof, or information; a set of such sheets

double-spacing in typing or handwriting a paper, leaving one line blank between every line of writing; writing on every second line

draft (n) [draft (v)] a version of a written document; may refer to the final or any preliminary version; writing a version of a written document

E

editing the stage of the composing process in which mechanical erors, such as spelling and grammar errors, are checked for and eliminated

edition the whole set of copies of a publication printed at one time in one form; later editions usually contain corrections and revisions of earlier ones

editor someone who prepares a document for publication by selecting, revising, correcting, and so on; someone in charge of the policies of all or part of a newspaper or publishing house

ellipsis the leaving out of part of a sentence, usually word(s) not essential for comprehension

ellipsis points marks used for indicating ellipsis; usually three successive periods [. . .]

encyclopedia a reference work with articles on many subjects; students often start with an encyclopedia article when seeking information on a possible term paper topic

endnote a brief written comment placed at the end of a text, but not forming part of the text itself; usually adds some information not directly connected with the argument of the text; similar to AFTERWORD

entry in an index or bibliography or list of items, all the information about an item such as a book or article

ERIC Abbreviation of "Educational Resources Information Center" [see: MICROFILM]

essay a short composition, usually from the author's point of view and usually literary in style

evidence the information on which a proof or judgement is based; an argumentative research paper must provide evidence in support of the claim it makes

expert person with a high degree of skill or specialized knowledge

exposition (n) [expository (adj)] a clear presentation of facts and argument; papers written for academic purposes are expository in style

extract part of a written composition; something taken out of or picked out of a larger unit

F

family name in an English language environment, the last name or surname; alphabetization in a catalog, index, or bibliography is based on the family name

file (n) [file (v)] a collection of papers or cards kept in systematic arrangement; the container of such a collection; in a computer information storage system, refers to any separately definable set of entries

final draft the version of a written work that is considered the end product of the composing process; the draft that a student hands in to an instructor or that a writer sends to a publisher

focus the main point of interest; in a paper, the thesis statement focuses on the main point; each paragraph also has a focus, often expressed in a topic sentence

footnote a note placed at the bottom of a page of writing or at the end of a paper, containing a comment or a reference

foreword a statement at the beginning of a text, but not part of the main text; often gives information about why and how the work was written; a preface; an introductory note before and separate from the text

formal conforming to stated and accepted conventions or rules; showing strict observance of correct forms, as determined by custom or regulation; a research paper is a formal presentation to a reader; opposite of "informal" (a letter to a good friend is normally informal); the language of a research paper is formal, in contrast to the language of casual conversation

format the visual layout, size, and shape of a publication; a plan for arranging parts of something in relation to other parts

free writing writing which is aimed at letting ideas flow freely out of the mind, without being blocked by thinking about spelling, grammar, punctuation; the purpose is to "discover" ideas; the writer usually writes non-stop for a fixed number of minutes; if ideas "dry up," the writer just keeps writing, letting any words or repetitions emerge onto the page; an excellent technique for overcoming writer's block; see DISCOVERY DRAFT and WRITER'S BLOCK

G

gazetteer geographic dictionary or index

given name a person's name other than the family name or surname; a name given at birth to a child by its parents; sometimes called the "first" or "Christian" name; the given name is never used for alphabetizing

glossary a collection of specialized terms, with explanation of their meanings in the specialized context

graph a visual display of how two sets of numbers are related to each other, such as a bar graph or line graph

H

handwriting writing done with the hand; the characteristic writing of a particular person

heading word, phrase or statement at the beginning of a section of writing, such as a chapter heading; headings are usually marked by underlining or being of a bigger or different type [see: CENTERED HEADING, SIDE HEADING, PARAGRAPH HEADING]

humanities philosophy, literature, and fine arts [contrast SOCIAL SCIENCES and SCIENCES]

I

indent to set in a line of typescript or handwriting from the margin; the first line of a paragraph is usually indented; all the lines of a long quotation are set in from the margin, forming a separate BLOCK

illustration clarification by use of example or pictures; an explanatory example, picture, photograph, or diagram

index an alphabetized listing of the names, places, and subjects in a printed work, giving the page on which each can be found; in English language publications, normally placed at the end of the text

interlibrary loan reference to the system by which an item not available in a library may be borrowed on behalf of a reader from some other library in the country

in-text documentation the type of documentation which uses parenthetical information in the text itself for references; the information in parentheses is used together with information in the bibliography; also called AUTHOR/DATE DOCUMENTATION

introduction in a composition, the first paragraph(s), usually giving some background and an indication of what will follow in the body; in a research paper, the introduction includes the thesis statement or statement of purpose; the term is sometimes used synonymously with PREFACE

issue a point of discussion; "at issue" = in dispute (e.g. The point at issue is clear.); "take issue with" = to disagree with (e.g. These two writers take issue with each other.)

italic having the quality of a typescript with letters slanting to the right, often used for emphasis or to distinguish foreign words; ''in italics'' = written in such typescript (*italics*); underlining is usually used as a handwritten or typed equivalent of what is in italics in a printed text

J

journal a specialized periodical, usually containing articles written by various authors; in a general sense, refers to newspapers and popular magazines, but has a more scholarly and academic connotation; the word is often used in the title of professional periodicals; most academic journals are published monthly, bimonthly, quarterly, or semi-annually

L

last name same as FAMILY NAME
legible clear enough to be read; opposite of ''illegible''
library a collection of publications, such as books, records, prints, and so on, used for reading or references; the place where such a collection is kept
Library of Congress classification system a way of arranging books in a library, with letters and numbers referring to subject areas; many college libraries use this system

A	General Works and Polygraphy
B	Philosophy and Religion
C	History and Auxiliary Sciences
D	History and Topography (except America)
E	America (general) and U.S. (general)
F	U.S. (local) and America except for the U.S.
G	Geography and Anthropology
H	Social Science
J	Political Science
K	Law
L	Education
M	Music
N	Fine Arts
P	Language and Literature
Q	Science
R	Medicine
S	Agriculture and Plant and Animal Industry
T	Technology
U	Military Science
V	Naval Science
Z	Bibliography and Library Science

These categories are further divided, with letters and numerical coding, into country, language used, type of literature, and period of literature. A librarian will help you find the exact coding of interest to you.

linking devices   same as TRANSITIONS

list   a written series of items, often arranged in a special order

literature (n) [literary (adj)]   all the written work produced in a given subject area; a long paper or dissertation usually includes a review of the relevant literature; imaginative or creative writing (as in the phrases "English Literature," "French literature," etc.); printed material of any kind; "literary" (adj) usually refers to imaginative or creative writing

loan   something lent for temporary use, as when a book is borrowed from a library

lower case   in reference to typescript or handwriting, small letters [contrast: UPPER CASE]

M   **magazine**   a periodical containing articles, stories, and so on; usually refers to more popular periodicals than the term JOURNAL

main idea   same as CONTROLLING IDEA

main idea statement   same as thesis statement; the sentence expressing the central idea, claim, or assertion

manuscript   a handwritten composition; a typewritten or handwritten version of a book, article, etc., especially the author's own copy, submitted for publication; handwriting as opposed to printing

margin   the blank space around the written on or printed area of a page; more often used for the blank space on each side than for the spaces above and below

microform   a way of photographing and storing documents in greatly reduced size; especially used for old, rare, or very large documents; some types of microform are: microfilm, microfiche, aperture card, microprint, and microcard; the ERIC (Educational Resources Information Center) collection is on microfiche and available in many college libraries; most type of microform can be photocopied using equipment located in the libraries

MLA   abbreviation of "Modern Language Association"; this association publishes a style guide used in some humanities

N   **narrow**   small or limited in scope; a research paper subject is normally narrow in scope, in order to make it manageable; a subject that is not narrow in scope is better dealt with in a book or dissertation; opposite of "wide" or "broad"

newspaper   a daily or weekly publication with articles on current affairs, news, and special features; usually contains advertising and usually printed on non-lasting paper; daily newspapers are not normally referred to as PERIODICALS

note   a brief written record; notes for a paper are of various types: personal opinion of writer, paraphrases and/or quotations from sources, summaries

note card   in research paper writing, usually refers to a file card adapted for use in making notes from written sources; such cards, as opposed to notes on regular-sized note paper, make it easier to change the order or grouping of information before writing a draft of a paper

note taking [also: "note making"]   the activity of recording in writing information from various sources

O   **open stacks**   library shelves open to borrowers; most college libraries have open stacks among which students may browse and from which they personally remove the books they want [contrast: CLOSED STACKS]

outline   a general description, plan or summary; in writing, usually refers to a plan of the content of the composition, in which no details are given; in such an outline numbers, letters and indentation are used to show the comparative importance of headings and subheadings, which in turn reflect the comparative importance of sections of the composition; a "temporary," "preliminary," or "working" outline is one which a writer prepares before the final draft as a means of organizing and stimulating thoughts on a subject

P   **pagination**   the numbering of pages; arrangement and numbering of pages in a book

pamphlet   a short composition or written information of various kinds published on a few sheets with no binding

paper   an essay, report, or scholarly composition

paragraph   a distinct unit of written text, having these characteristics: unit of thought, usually several sentences, started on a new line, first line indented

paragraph heading   a heading placed at the beginning of a paragraph, forming part of the paragraph, with the usual indenting in the first line; used with centered and side headings in long papers [compare: CENTERED HEADING and SIDE HEADING]

paraphrase   restatement in different words, without change of meaning, often aimed at clarifying the meaning; paraphrasing is important in notetaking for a research paper, because it enables the writer to report someone else's ideas without lengthy direct quotation and without running the risk of plagiarism

periodical   a publication issued at regular intervals of more than one day

photocopy   photographic reproduction; when making notes for a paper, it is sometimes helpful to photocopy a few pages, especially of charts, graphs, and diagrams; copyright law permits such copying for private study and research

phrase   group of words smaller than a clause; expression in words; manner of expression

plagiarism (n) [plagiarize (v)]   stealing and using the ideas or writings of someone else as if they are one's own

planning   the part of the composing process in which schemes, outlines and limitations or necessities of the discourse are established; planning occurs throughout the process and at many levels, from individual sounds and words to paragraphs and sections of text

preface   an introduction, not part of the main text, to a book, speech, or long piece of writing

preliminary   coming before the main action; preparatory, as in "preliminary draft" or "preliminary thesis statement"; the preliminary versions of written material are usually aimed at helping the writer organize ideas and information; to produce a good final draft, several preliminary versions are usually necessary at different stages of the process

prewriting   the stage of the composing process before any writing is done; during this stage the writer thinks about possible subjects and ways of dealing with the subject and the writing task to be accomplished is defined and clarified in the writer's mind

primary source   original supplier of information, who has directly and personally observed what makes up that information [compare: SECONDARY SOURCE]

print   to make multiple copies of a publication, usually by a mechanical method with ink on paper; to produce for publication; to write in a manner typical of printed materials, such as block letters or separate small letters

proceedings   the events or activities of a situation; the proceedings of a conference are sometimes published in book form, as a collection of the papers or talks given at the meeting

professional journal   periodical concerned with the interests of a distinct group of highly trained specialists

project   a task requiring special effort and planning; a term paper is often referred to as a "term project," even though "project" usually refers to a wider range of activities, not all of which must involve writing

proof (n) [prove (v)]   evidence showing that something is true; a line of reasoning showing that an argument is valid

proofreading   reading some written work in order to correct mistakes; for a research paper, synonymous with EDITING

proposal   something put forward for consideration; a research paper ending with a recommendation of further action or research may sometimes be called a "proposal"; a graduate student's written submission of a detailed plan for thesis or dissertation research

publication   something prepared and issued for public distribution, often printed or written

publication manual   same as STYLE GUIDE

publisher   the person, organization, or business unit preparing material for public distribution

punctuation   the use of conventional marks (such as periods, commas, and quotation marks) in writing or printing to separate units and clarify meaning

Q   **quarterly**   published four times per year, as in "quarterly journal"

questionnaire   a printed form containing a set of questions, used frequently in surveys

quote (v) [quotation (n)] to repeat or copy someone else's words; to cite or refer to for illustration or proof

R **reference** another work mentioned in a book or article; the note in a publication that mentions another work; when listed, references are placed at the end of the text; a reference list normally includes only those works directly referred to in the text [compare: BIBLIOGRAPHY]

reference book in a library, a book that cannot be borrowed; reference books, usually including such items as dictionaries, encyclopedias, and catalogs, are kept in a separate area of a library

reference librarian a librarian assigned to the task of helping users to make best use of the library by answering questions about the card catalog, helping to find books, assisting with locating materials for specific research interests; usually stationed at a library's "reference desk"

report (n) (v) an organized account of something; a research paper or term paper is called a "report" when it is a presentation of what others have said, written, or found out; this type of paper does not include the writer's point of view or the writer's own argument on the topic reported [compare: ARGUMENTATIVE RESEARCH PAPER, CRITIQUE]

reprint (n) (v) a publication printed again

research (n) (v) investigation; systematic, scientific study to discover facts; scholarly inquiry

research paper a long written composition based on systematic search through published information, followed by a careful use of the information either as a report or, with the inclusion of argument and discussion from the writer's point of view, in a paper that tries to persuade the reader to see the issue as the writer does

reserve book room a room in a college library for books required by many readers in connection with a specific course; the instructor places certain books "on reserve," to be used only in the library and not to be borrowed for long periods, so that all readers have access to them

resource something available for use; a supply that can be drawn on for use

review (n) (v) a report or essay giving an evaluation of a work or performance as in a "book review" or "film review"; re-examination; inspection or examination with intention of criticism or correction

revision (n) [revise (v)] the part of the composing process in which a way of expressing something is reviewed and changed; revision can occur at all levels; word, clause, sentence, paragraph, or whole composition; a newly edited version of a text; revised thesis statements, outlines, or drafts may be part of the composing process for a research paper; in general, a change or modification in something

rhetoric the art of effective expression in speech or writing

rhetorical pattern a specific way of arranging information and ideas in a text, such as comparison, contrast, classification, division, process, cause and effect, definition; very few compositions (other than school exercises) consist of only one pattern; a research paper will usually make use of many rhetorical patterns

Roman numerals the symbols (based on letters of the Roman alphabet) I, V, X, L, C, D, M used to express numbers; frequently used to number those pages in a book that come before the body of the text [compare: ARABIC NUMERALS]

rough draft a preliminary written version of something

S **scan** see SKIM

scholarly journal periodical concerned with the interests of scholars and academics

sciences disciplines (such as chemistry and physics) in which knowledge is obtained through observation, description, experimental investigation, and theoretical explanation of natural phenomena; contrast HUMANITIES and SOCIAL SCIENCES

search term a word or phrase under which material is classified in information indexing systems and which can be used in looking for information; researchers develop lists of search terms to locate references in card catalogs, specialized subject indexes, journal indexes, and computerized information storage systems

secondary source an indirect supplier of information; for example, a report by someone on an experiment carried out by someone else, is a secondary source, but a report written by the experimenter himself is a primary source [compare: PRIMARY SOURCE]

see (see also) instruction to the user of a catalog or index to refer to another relevant entry; indication of a CROSS-REFERENCE

semi-annual happening or issued twice a year; same as "biannual" [contrast: "biennial"—every two years]

sentence a unit of language consisting of a word or group of words with at least one subject and a finite verb or verb phrase

side heading a heading placed at the extreme left of a line, starting at the margin; used with centered headings in papers that are not very short [compare: CENTERED HEADING and PARAGRAPH HEADING]

single spacing in typing or handwriting, leaving no blank lines between each line of writing; writing on every line

skim to read quickly, looking only for main points; researchers often read books and articles this way to decide whether a source will be of use in their projects; synonymous with "scan," in the opinion of some reading specialists, but others differentiate "skimming" and "scanning" according to whether the reader is looking for all the main points or for one specific piece of information (texts differ from each other as to which word is applied to which way of reading)

small letter   a letter of the alphabet written in its smaller form, as compared to its corresponding capital letter; a lower-case letter

social sciences   disciplines related to the study of human society, its organization and interactions (usually includes sociology, psychology, education); contrast HUMANITIES and SCIENCES

source   origin; starting point; a writer's "sources" are the books, articles, interviews, and so on from which information is obtained

spacing   in typing or handwriting, refers to how many lines, if any, are left blank between each line of writing; organizing or arranging with spaces in between areas of writing, graphics, and so on

specialized   devoted to a particular branch of study or research, as in "specialized index" or "specialized journal"

stacks   the area of a library in which books are shelved; shelves

style   the way in which something is said or done; the characteristic features of literary or artistic expression; a customary manner of presenting printed or written material, including spelling, format, typography, punctuation, usage, and so on

style guide   a printed manual that gives a writer information on conventions of usage, format, punctuation, footnoting, bibliographies, and so on; various scholarly organizations and journals have their particular requirements and publish their own guides; same as PUBLICATION MANUAL

subheading   a heading of secondary importance; usually written in smaller type or placed less prominently than a major heading [see: HEADING]

subject   an area of study; a course; a topic about which something is said or done

subject card   in a card catalog, the type of card alphabetized according to what it deals with, as opposed to AUTHOR CARD or TITLE CARD

summary (n) [summarize (v)]   a shortened version of a text, including only the main points; a condensation of ideas; abstract

surname   same as FAMILY NAME or LAST NAME

survey (n) (v)   examining or looking at in a comprehensive way; a general or comprehensive view

synonym   a word having a meaning similar to that of another; opposite of "antonym"

synthesis (n) [synthesize (v)]   combining separate elements to form a unified whole

T

table   an orderly display of data, usually in rows and columns; an abbreviated list, as of contents

term paper   a written school assignment to be prepared during the course of one whole term and therefore normally much longer than written assignments for which only a few days or a few weeks are available; frequently, the term paper is a research paper or report; sometimes called a "term project"

text   the wording or words of something written or printed; the body of a composition, as opposed to its preface, footnotes, bibliography, or appendices; textbook

theme   a short written composition; the subject of an artistic work; a topic of discourse or discussion

theory (n) [theorize (v)]   hypothesis or supposition to account for something; system of rules and principles; rules and reasoning and general principles as opposed to practice

thesaurus   a book of selected words, especially synonyms and antonyms; often useful to a researcher in establishing SEARCH TERMS

thesis   an assertion supported by argument; a dissertation resulting from original research, especially the kind required for an academic degree, as in ''master's thesis'' or ''doctoral thesis''

thesis statement   in a paper, the sentence embodying its central idea or claim

title   name of book or article

title card   in a card catalog, a card alphabetized according to the title of the work, as opposed to AUTHOR CARD or SUBJECT CARD

title page   in reference to a research paper, same as COVER PAGE; in reference to a book, the page on which the title is written together with the names of author and publisher (before the copyright page and body of the text)

topic   subect of discourse or composition; a ''general topic'' covers a wide area of knowledge or study, too wide for a short research paper; a ''narrowed topic'' refers to one small aspect of an area of knowledge or study and is appropriate for a short research paper, especially one to be written in a short period of time, such as one term or semester

topic sentence   in a paragraph, a sentence expressing the scope or main idea of that paragraph

transcribe   to copy out in handwriting or in typing; to write out fully, as from notes

transitions   words, phrases, clauses, sentences, or paragraphs that provide connections between parts of a text, as between sentences, paragraphs, or major sections; transitions may be contrasted with expressions of content, which are the elements joined by the transitions; transitions are also called ''connectors'', ''linking devices'', or ''cohesive devices''

typewrite   to write with a typewriter, as opposed to ''handwrite''

U **underline**   to draw a line under; in handwritten or typed text, underlining is used as an equivalent of what in a printed text is in italics.

unity   the quality of having all parts contribute to the single effect of the whole; in a paragraph with this quality, all the sentences support the controlling idea or topic sentence; in a composition that has unity, all the paragraphs contribute to supporting the thesis statement

unpublished   not made public in a book, journal, or by other means of reproduction; may describe a manuscript in private circulation; often describes a dissertation or thesis

upper case   in reference to typescript or handwriting, capital letters [contrast: LOWER CASE]

V   **valid**   in reference to an argument, following logical steps of reasoning

vertical file index   a library catalog listing materials (such as pamphlets and advertising brochures) that are neither books nor periodicals and which therefore do not appear in the card catalog or periodicals indexes

volume   a book; one book in a set; a collection of written or printed sheets bound together

W   **word**   a meaningful unit of language made up of sounds or written symbols; words are usually written with spaces between them

wording   the manner of expressing in words

wordy   using more words than necessary

writer's block   the state of mind a writer gets into in which it seems impossible to get started or write any more or think of anything to write; writers have various techniques to get past this: some use free writing; some work on a different section of the paper; some take a break of a few hours; some read and re-read what they have already written; some talk their ideas into a tape recorder and play this back; see FREE WRITING and DISCOVERY DRAFT

writing   the stage of the composing process in which text is drafted; also used to refer to the composing process as a whole; also refers to the physical act of putting words on a page; handwriting

Y   **yearbook**   a book published every year, containing information about the previous year

Index

(Except in a few cases, entries in the Glossary are not included in this Index.)

Reader of student paper, 64–65, 66–67, 102
Readers' Guide to Periodical Literature: description of entries and examples, 10–11; exercises, 11, 12
Reference source: card catalog as, 16; defined, 16; examples, 17–18; people as, 17; types of, 16–17. *See also* Indexes; *Readers' Guide to Periodical Literature*
References: distinguished from bibliography, 70; examples of APA style, 21–27; exercises, 28–29; format, 70; number of, 98; for preliminary bibliography, 19–20, 101; purpose, 68
Report, 1, 100–01. *See also* Research paper
Research paper: defined, 1, 103–04; steps in, 2, 66–67; structure of, 3, 104; types of, 1. *See also* Student research paper samples
Revision, 121. *See also* Drafting process
Rhetorical patterns. *See* Organization of ideas.
Rough draft. *See* Drafting process

Scientific style: student research paper sample in, 90–96

Student research paper samples: in APA format, 73–80; in MLA format, 81–89; in scientific format, 90–96
Style guide: choice of, 98; this textbook as, 98. *See also* APA style; MLA style; Scientific style
Subject: choice of, 5; examples, 6; interest in, 5; practicality in choice of, 5. *See also* Narrowing of subject

Tables, 70–71
Text of the paper, 62–63
Thesis statement, preliminary: defined, 30–31; examples for argumentative paper, 31–32; examples for report, 32; examples with outlines, 36–37; exercise, 32–34
Title, 62
Typing of papers: effect on reader, 98. *See also* Student research paper samples

Writer's block, 59, 125
Writing process. *See* Drafting process

Questionnaire

To the Instructor and Student

Books in this series are revised to meet the needs of users. Your recommendations about possible improvements are highly valued. Please take a few minutes to complete this questionnaire. Return it to:

English Language Institute
2816 Cathedral of Learning
University of Pittsburgh
Pittsburgh, PA 15260

Your school: _____

School location (city, state): _____

Course in which the book was used: _____

Check one: Instructor ☐   Student ☐

Instructors, check here to receive an examination copy of a revised edition of this book. (Examination copies are sent on a 60-day trial basis and charged to the individual until the book is paid for, is returned in saleable condition, or an order for ten or more copies is received from the individual's college bookstore.): ☐

Instructor's name and mailing address for examination copy of a revised edition:

Name _____

Institution _____

Address _____

City _____ State _____ Zip

Please write here any comments or suggestions for improvement of the book:

_____

_____

_____

_____

_____

Please turn over

CUT HERE

WRITING A RESEARCH PAPER

Place check marks in the appropriate spaces to rate each unit.

		Very Useful	Useful	Not Useful
Unit 1	Writing Research Papers			
Unit 2	Choosing a Subject			
Unit 3	Using the Library			
Unit 4	Narrowing the Focus			
Unit 5	Preliminary Survey of Reference Sources			
Unit 6	Preliminary Bibliography			
Unit 7	Preliminary Thesis Statement			
Unit 8	Preliminary Outline			
Unit 9	Plagiarism			
Unit 10	Note Taking			
Unit 11	Revised Thesis Statement			
Unit 12	Revised Outline			
Unit 13	Sample Draft			
Unit 14	Preliminary Draft			
Unit 15	Final Draft			
Unit 16	APA Editorial Style			
Unit 17	MLA and Scientific Formats			
Unit 18	Frequent Student Questions			
Glossary				

Thank you for completing this questionnaire. Your cooperation is greatly appreciated.

CUT HERE